S

Second Marriage

*Guidelines on remarriage
and Step-parenting*

Merrilyn Williams

KINGSWAY PUBLICATIONS
EASTBOURNE

Biblical quotations are from the
New International Version (NIV) © International Bible
Society 1973, 1978, 1984
and the Authorised Version (Crown copyright)

Front cover photo: The Image Bank
Front cover design by W James Hammond

British Library Cataloguing in Publication Data

Williams, Merrilyn
   Second marriage.
   1. Remarriage—Christian viewpoints
   I. Title
   261.8'3584

   ISBN 0-86065-733-7

Printed in Great Britain for
KINGSWAY PUBLICATIONS LTD
1 St Anne's Road, Eastbourne, E Sussex BN21 3UN by
Courier International Ltd, Tiptree, Essex
Typeset by Nuprint Ltd, Harpenden, Herts AL5 4SE.

Acknowledgements

My grateful thanks to all those who have been generous enough to share their stories, and selfless enough to be honest about their own problems, weaknesses and failures. All names and some details have been changed in order to protect their privacy and that of their families.

I very much appreciate also the two solicitors who, as friends, advised me and checked over the various legal matters mentioned in Chapter ten. They are: Stephen C G Govier of Govier and Govier, Exeter; and Alistair Harper of Torquay.

My love and thanks go also to my family: my husband Paul for his love, patience, advice and support, not to mention all that he does in a practical sense in correcting my spelling mistakes; to my children who have all helped to make possible the happiness and harmony of our step-family; and to my parents for their love and encouragement, without which I should not have had the courage to try again.

Most of all, to the Lord who is all-forgiving, all-accepting and all-loving, to whom I owe all that I am, all that I have and all that I hope for.

Contents

Foreword by Canon Max Wigley   9

1 Viewing the Site   11
   surveying the situation;
   statistics and testimony

2 Preparing the Ground   27
   inner healing

3 Family Foundations   43
   a sensitive approach to breaking the news

4 Establishing an Equitable Economy   61
   budgetting income;
   maintenance;
   working wives;
   wills

5 Forming the Framework and...   81
   marriage as the base of the family;
   accepting one another;
   having realistic expectations

6 Putting It in Place   93
   ongoing healing;
   uprooting—new home/town fellowship;
   creating time alone;
   showing affection;
   submission/commitment

7   The Living Quarters   111
     acceptance in the step-relationships;
     getting used to one another;
     facing the limitations;
     jealousies;
     putting the past into perspective

8   Problems with the Fittings   127
     coping with conflict;
     tracing the source;
     the problem of guilt;
     letting go

9   Penalty Clauses—Discipline   143
     mutual respect—the basis of authority;
     punishment and affection;
     problems not exclusive to the stepfamily

10 Entrances and exits   161
     access with absent parent;
     split loyalties;
     manipulative behaviour;
     spite/insecurity;
     meeting your spouse's 'ex';
     access with absent children, legalities—
     changing names

11 Beyond the Boundaries   181
     weddings;
     Christmas;
     coming-of-age;
     grandparents;
     new baby

12 Windows on the World   201
     living with a mistake;
     dealing with guilt;
     second-class citizens?
     how the stepfamily is viewed by world/
     church/school

Appendix   215

Foreword

This book is long overdue and I am thankful to Merrilyn Williams for writing on such an important subject. She has successfully and realistically tackled the problems faced by people who remarry following either divorce or the death of their first partner. The fact that she has been through the sadness of a broken marriage and entered a new marriage, together with her children from the first marriage, means that she knows from experience what she is talking about. Her case studies of other couples in a similar position add to the scope of the book.

The book is a thorough attempt to look at all the areas faced by a couple when they become step-parents. It is naturally written from a Christian perspective but does not attempt to give glib answers to complicated problems. Whilst looking to our Lord for help and guidance there is no sense of pious platitudes being given to solve what *is* very difficult.

It has taken years for Christians to begin to admit that some Christian marriages do fail and end in divorce, like so many other marriages. Those concerned have to live through the pain and bereavement of that failure. As well as coping with the sense of loss and guilt this causes, many have to suffer rejection by their fellow believers at a time when they most need love and support.

Whilst our Lord taught that his will is that marriage is for life, he also forgives us when we fail to reach that ideal. The New Testament knows nothing about forgiveness without a new beginning, praise God for that. People who therefore remarry have to live with the scars of that broken marriage—and their children do too.

This book will help such people to be prepared for some of the problems they will most likely face. It will also help those who have a good marriage to be more understanding of the difficulties of those who are, in the grace of God, starting again.

Canon Max Wigley

I

Viewing the Site

The little church was decorated with a profusion of summer garden flowers: roses, lilies and hydrangeas. Apart from the bridal posy and buttonholes for the groom and best man, Penny and Maurice had been unable to afford a florist's bill. But what they lacked in worldly wealth was well compensated for in the treasure of their love—for each other, their families and friends.

Heart pounding, Penny took in the scene before her. It seemed, as she came down the aisle on her father's arm, that there was scarcely a pew vacant. It was touching to know how far some of the guests had travelled to witness this moment, especially as few were included on the guest list for the reception. Reaching the altar steps Penny stole a glance at her husband-to-be as they stood side-by-side, and suddenly the nervousness she'd been feeling vanished.

And then it was over: a few snatches of hymns, vows made in a daze, a half-remembered reading, and the merest thread of the sermon. Up the aisle they trod, and out into the sunshine—a hot, relentless, burning brightness. Cameras clicked. Confetti was thrown. The uninvited guests were gathered up by the bride's father to be taken home for the reception.

Penny was glad of the broad-brimmed hat which she'd swathed with a piece of Brussels lace—legacy of a redun-

dant Christening robe. It at least afforded her face some
protection from the glare as they made their way on foot
across the village green to her parents' home. But Maurice
plucked uncomfortably with one finger at his tightly but-
toned collar and tie.

It was not only the physical discomfort of being so
overdressed; both were acutely embarrassed at the
incongruity of the situation. Suddenly aware of the attention they were receiving as bride and groom amongst the
scantily-clad holidaymakers, they quickened their pace,
hastening to receive the wedding guests.

The names of Penny and Maurice were now linked
irrevocably together in matrimony. But they were a married couple with a difference. For in that service of con-
nubial unity, they had joined the ranks of second-time-
rounders—or at least Penny had—and become one of a
series of statistics.

Maurice had been a bachelor. Penny, on the other
hand, was a divorcee—one of the many. For every wedding conducted in the UK, a third end in divorce, sometimes for the second or third time! In fact, of the total
number of marriages made in any one year, rather less
than two thirds are for the first time on both sides. The
media spell out the startling statistics in no uncertain
terms: an estimated six million people now belong to stepfamilies with children under the age of sixteen.

Yet Penny and Maurice were in illustrious company.
Their wedding had followed hard on the heels of the most
fairytale romance of the century—the marriage of Lady
Diana Spencer to her Prince Charming. And only shortly
afterwards came the nuptials of the Duke and Duchess of
York. In both instances the two young women who
exchanged the age-old vows of eternal fidelity with their
princes, were themselves the innocent victims of one of the
most prolific problems of our times—the broken home
and Stepfamily Syndrome.

As Penny and Maurice had exchanged rings in the tiny Baptist church in the heart of the West Country, Penny couldn't help wondering how his mother would have viewed such 'goings on' had she been one of the congregation of family and friends. Second marriages might now be a 'sign of the times', but before her demise a quarter of a century ago, they were most certainly not. At least, not in the devout Christian quarters from which she hailed.

Yet her death, when Maurice was only in his teens, had itself been instrumental in producing a second marriage and stepfamily situation. Like most men, Maurice's father had found the prospect of living alone somewhat daunting, to say the least. He'd remained a widower only a short time before presenting Maurice and his brother with their new step mother. But then widowhood has never been deemed a bar on remarriage.

The reasons for remarriage are few. Divorce or death constitute the only possibilities open to those living in any civilisation governed by the laws of monogamy. Any other reason would be deemed bigamy, a criminal offence.

But though the law may allow remarriage after divorce, the church—corporately and individually—remains divided on the issue.

'Now don't you worry about girl-friends,' Maurice's mother had always told him. 'The Lord will find the right wife for you.'

Faithfully he'd hung on, through thirty-six years of bachelorhood and numerous light-hearted romances. Penny found it humbling to think that if that prophecy were to be believed, she was the 'right wife' whom the Lord had found. But would Maurice's mother have accepted his choice, Penny wondered? Would she, in fact, have seen that choice as being the Lord's, or merely an error on Maurice's part?

Be that as it may, they had no qualms on that score. Despite Penny's desire to adhere to the lifelong vows of her first marriage, she'd discovered, as have others, that it takes two to keep a relationship intact. And she'd come to realise too, that though others may moralise, God alone is our judge.[1] What a comforting thought! To know that she had no need to defend herself against the criticism of her neighbour, for only the Lawgiver knows when we transgress.

He alone knows the heart, that innermost part where choices are weighed in the balance with motive, and decisions are finally made. His Fatherly heart is merciful toward his children, loving and compassionate. Even where mistakes have been made, he delights to turn them to his purposes, to bring blessings to his children and glory to his name, by 'working all things together for good.'[2]

Crumbling homes on unstable foundations

Like it or not, divorce and remarriage are facts of life and it behoves us, as God's children, to show the same understanding and compassion. It is futile to moralise, profitless to judge. Broken and rebuilt homes affect a large proportion of the population and are increasingly encroaching upon the domains of 'respectable' Christianity.

Statistically, the vast majority of remarriages take place early on, with the largest number of women marrying for the second time before their twenty-fourth birthday. A significant proportion of remarriages occur after two or more previous attempts.

With more and more children growing up in unstable home backgrounds, the chances are that with no other example or teaching they too will contract unstable marriages.

The divine architect

God may hate divorce[3], but in working all things together for good, he uses even this tragedy to further his kingdom.

We see, in fellowships up and down the country, previously unchurched folk who through the trauma of divorce and remarriage have turned to Jesus in their hurt and confusion. What a golden opportunity for Christians to show that understanding, love and meeting of their special needs, not to mention the teaching pertinent to a stepfamily situation.

A divorcee myself, we became one of the stepfamily statistics when I married my second husband, Paul. With the Church of England's policy of no remarriage after divorce, most take place, as ours did, in the free church. Paul had been a member of a Baptist church for more than twenty years, so it was a relief to know, that although a member of the Anglican church myself, our local Baptist minister was more than happy to marry us.

'Knowing your background as I do,' he had told me when his wife and I met up for our regular interdenominational bible studies, 'I'd have no hesitation in remarrying you.'

That remarriage was to prove a blessing beyond my wildest dreams. In God's hands the hurts of the past were healed. Taking the raw materials of human error, mistaken judgement, even wilful disobedience, he showed himself able, not simply to rebuild a life, but to turn ugliness into beauty, restoring self-worth and a sense of purpose in place of humiliation and rejection. Under his gentle guidance during the following years, my children and I were to come to know the truth of having restored to us the years that the locusts had eaten.[4]

And as it was for us, so it is for others. We may not like what is happening all around us in this twentieth century. With the devaluation and destruction of all we once held dear—the sanctity of marriage, the stability of the family unit, the security of our nation's children—we may fear for the survival of the human race.

But we have a God who surveys the war-torn devastation of civilisation, the bomb-sites of individual lives, and sees in them the potential for fine new buildings to arise from the ashes of despair. The Divine Architect—given free rein—fashions bricks from the rubble of broken relationships, builds blocks from the clay of a broken spirit, and binds them together with the mortar of his love to create within us a temple fit for the habitation of his Holy Spirit.

A firm foundation

Amongst those who, in sharing their stories with us confirmed this truth, the variety was infinite. Some were back-slidden Christians brought back into a new relationship with the Lord. Others, living seemingly successful lives by the world's standards, found the secret yearning of their hearts fulfilled as they came to know Jesus for the first time. In place of the shifting sands of broken relationships, he alone was to be their rock.

Barrie and Margot were one couple. Outwardly, with their respective partners from their first marriages, all seemed well. Barrie, a quiet and dependable husband, earned a good living by anyone's standards. His eight-year-old marriage to Jayne wasn't superb, but it wasn't too bad. They seemed happy enough—or so he thought.

He and Jayne spent a good deal of time in the company of their friends, Margot and Jeremy. They were near neighbours after all, and the children all got on well together; it was natural to share outings, and meals in one another's homes as a foursome. Perhaps, in hindsight, it was the more exuberant Jayne and Jeremy who set the pace, but who would have guessed the outcome...

Quiet dependable Barrie, and thoughtful, cautious Margot were devastated when they learned the truth behind the foursome friendship. For Jeremy and Jayne the stolen moments of a full-blown affair no longer seemed sufficient. They left their respective partners, and their respective children, and moved away to set up home together.

Barrie couldn't believe it. Neither could Margot, though in truth, there had long been something missing in her twelve-year marriage to Jeremy.

'But nothing I could put my finger on,' she told me. 'There was nothing basically wrong. It was just that I felt, somehow, rather a failure.'

Barrie, on the other hand, felt utterly rejected by Jayne.

It seemed natural, having a shared experience such as this, and having known one another so long, that Margot and Barrie should comfort one another.

'We sort of helped one another,' Margot smiled affectionately in Barrie's direction. 'I had to collect my kids from school, so it was just as easy to have Barrie's as well and keep them at home until he got back from work.' She shrugged a shoulder as if to make light of her action. 'And he obviously helped me,' she continued, 'cutting the lawn, mending a fuse…'

Privately, Margot blamed Jayne, of course. 'Looking back, it was obvious,' she recalled. 'She was out to get Jeremy right from the word go.' Anger and resentment had built up in her, fuelled by Barrie's own feelings of rebuff from Jayne.

Marriage between Margot and Barrie seemed to follow on inevitably, about two years after their divorces went through and their first partners had married one another. 'There was no earth-shattering romance,' they admitted. But a quiet assurance that they felt safe together and enjoyed being with one another seemed a good basis for their new partnership.

They set up home with Margot's two toddlers, and two of Barrie's three school-age children. The youngest went to Jayne, his mother, now married to Jeremy, Margot's ex-husband.

An intricate set-up! And one that was not to be without further complications. But God took the tangled mess and began to unravel it. Although neither Barrie nor Margot were Christians at the time, both intermittently attended church.

Margot had been a confirmed atheist at the time of her first marriage and for years after. Now, through increasing difficulties in their step family situation, she reached her lowest point—that point of despair and need where we realise we've run out of ourselves and that there's nothing left but to cast ourselves on the only One who can help.

'But I didn't even believe he existed!' Margot told me in her quiet way. 'Eventually, I just said, "if you're really real, you'll have to show me." ' A smile lit her brown eyes, curving her lips into a mischievous grin. 'And he did!' she concluded simply.

Her commitment to Jesus was soon succeeded by that of her husband Barrie. Three of the five children followed suit, and ultimately, through the witness of his daughter, Margot's first husband was also converted. From the ugly mess created by 'the world, the flesh and the devil', God made something beautiful; something of blessing to those involved; and something glorifying to his name.

* * * * * *

The set-up was rather less complicated in the case of Isobel and Warren. She had been a Christian for years when her policeman husband left her and the children for another woman. Subsequently, Isobel met Warren through friends, and though he was not a Christian, the attraction was mutual. But with one failed marriage behind her, she was not about to enter into another— especially when Warren didn't even share her faith!

After some months of seeing one another, Isobel felt they should not continue the relationship. Warren went abroad. But still he couldn't forget. He knew Isobel was the girl for him—no matter what. He returned to England, found the Lord Jesus for himself and made a firm commitment.

Still, Isobel held out. Still she was unsure. Warren might now share her faith, and it was true they enjoyed fellowship together, but still there was the question of age, the fact that he was some years her junior. Then again, there was the matter of her having had a hysterectomy. Warren was young, virile and single. Could he really accept an older wife, and the fact of never having a family of his own, other than Isobel's girls?

He could and did. Today they are a united family group, with a dynamic spiritual input into their church fellowship. Once again the Lord showed how he could triumph, bringing victory out of doubt and despair.

* * * * * *

Perhaps one of the most exciting testimonies of God's greatness in seeking us out in the devastation of our lives, and working even the messiest circumstances together to create something good, comes from Simon and Ros. Needless to say, they also have the most complex relationships.

A shrewd businessman and charismatic personality, Simon had for many years known an emptiness in his life which longed to be filled. His search had led him through numerous philosophies, cults and sects—and through the divorce courts not once, but twice—all before his thirtieth birthday!

With the two children of his first marriage living with their mother, that still left two tiny tots in his care when his second wife left. 'She just walked out and abandoned them,' he recalled, but without a trace of bitterness. 'I wasn't about to have them taken away from me and put into care, but I couldn't run my business and look after them myself.'

'So how did you cope?' I asked him.

Simon's blue eyes lit up. 'My mother came in every day and took care of them,' he said, 'She was marvellous really, but eventually even she couldn't cope.'

Ill health and old age caught up with Simon's parents, making it increasingly difficult for the arrangement to continue. When, through his job, he met Ros, all his needs seemed to be answered in her. Young, attractive and single, romance soon blossomed between them, and within a short time she willingly moved in to be 'mother' to the two little ones. For nearly two years they lived happily together.

'Ros was so lovely,' Simon recalled with a far-away look, 'not just to look at—she was everything a bloke would want in a wife. But something was dead inside me.'

After all the trauma of two broken marriages, Simon had been close to a nervous breakdown. His affair with Ros had been the best thing that had happened to him, yet he seemed unable to respond. This third relationship seemed threatened too.

'We had no money,' he continued, 'but we booked a holiday in America. I wanted desperately to love Ros, but couldn't. We were going to have the holiday of a lifetime then call it a day.' He shrugged his shoulders as if recalling his despair.

'It was stepping out of the ordinary—seeing myself 3,000 miles from home... I cracked, and begged Ros not to leave me. It all flooded out—the hurt and rejection.

'My sister had a lovely family and that broke me. There I was on tranquillisers and I thought I was going to die. I thought God was going to punish me.' Simon lapsed into silence.

'Was that your first spiritual awareness then?' I prompted him.

He nodded. His sister was a Jehovah's Witness, and he had himself looked into every religion, cult and ism.

'I knew I had to seek,' he said, 'and then I would find. When it happened, I had a really dramatic encounter with the Lord. I was delivered on the spot, without realising it, of all sorts of things. And I knew I'd been saved.'

But Simon's conversion put paid to his domestic arrangement with Ros! Finding that the inner emptiness, which had continued throughout their relationship, could be filled only with Jesus, he realised his search was now over. Nothing else had satisfied him in the way that he now found the Lord was able, and he willingly gave over his life, seeking salvation and forgiveness from his Saviour, and direction for the future from his Lord.

The church he joined happened to be the same one of which I was a member. I remember vividly the amazement written upon his face as he came along to house-group for the first time. 'I never expected Christians to be so ordinary, and able to enjoy life,' he confessed in his usual forthright manner.

But his new-found faith and the counsel of others was soon to upset the applecart! After talking with the elders of the fellowship, Simon felt that though the children should not again be deprived of a mother, he would have to make it clear that he could no longer live as man and wife with Ros.

Moving out of the bedroom, yet continuing to live intimately in the same house with someone you love can be no easy matter.

'I couldn't understand what he was on about,' Ros later admitted. 'Actually, I felt quite hurt and rejected. Simon just didn't seem to want me any more.'

It is to her credit, and the grace of God, that though

determined not to be 'got at' by religion herself, Ros stayed on to care for the children.

'I was determined not to get involved with all this church and Jesus business just because Simon was,' she laughed, 'in fact I was most reluctant even to think about it.'

But despite digging in her heels, the Lord continued to seek her out, until eventually she too knew the salvation to be found in Jesus.

Her ultimate conversion, their marriage—the third for Simon—and the addition of two further children in their lives, are a living testimony to the love and faithfulness of God.

******

Other stories, though less dramatic, are no less a blessing from God. Leslie and Laura were both Christians of many years' standing when they met. He spied her when as a member of a visting choir, she sang Christmas carols at his church. From then on he had eyes for no one else and romance blossomed over the after-service mince pies.

Laura was single, but Leslie's first marriage had ended in divorce when his wife had left him some years previously. His two girls were in their teens when he met and married Laura. With a Christian wife to encourage him now, Leslie's somewhat passive faith took on a new dynamic, and to add to their blessing they now have two little girls of their own.

Max and Cathy were also of mature years and faith when they married years after Max's divorce. Though single herself, unlike Laura, Cathy decided motherhood was not for her. She contented herself with being thrust, prematurely, into the role of stepgrandmother.

Doreen had been widowed for a number of years before marrying Jeff, a divorcee. In their situation there were children on both sides, all well into teenage and adult-hood, though one was still dependent.

In yet another couple's situation, Maureen's marriage to Bryan was further complicated by a dependent adopted child, as well as two adult offspring and a grandchild. Though both mature Christians, Bryan was some years Maureen's junior, and this was his first marriage—a tremendous responsibility to take on, and sadly one of the few with persistently unresolved problems. But they're still working at it and receiving counselling.

The variations are endless, with one or both divorced, single or widowed, or any combination thereof. In some cases the husband is younger than the wife. The numbers of children, their gender and age increase the diversity, as does the mixture of those living at home, and those who live with the other parent, but make periodic sojourns into the home of the step-family. Such children may, in fact, have two stepfamilies, with step-brothers and sisters on both sides, and/or the addition of half-siblings.

Building a kingdom of caring

It's not good enough to push the recognition of such families, ostrich-like, out of sight and mind. The fact is that, like it or not, they exist, are on the increase, and are appearing with more and more frequency in the church. Nor is simple awareness enough. The situation demands understanding and compassion. It should not surprise Christians to find stepfamilies in the Body of Christ. They are people who are bruised, broken and battle-weary— the very folk whom Jesus came to save and to heal.*

Their inclusion in the midst of the family of God indicates the unchanging love of the Lord. Though he may hate divorce, and indeed does, there is ample evidence in

---

* For more about the church's attitudes, see final chapter.

the testimonies of those quoted above, to indicate that he can and does use it as a means of bringing its victims to a saving knowledge of Christ. Nor is this confined to the divorced. Many a widow or widower can testify that it was the need to know the destiny of their loved one that drove them to seek the Lord for themselves.

Throughout his life here on earth, Jesus consistently met people at their point of need. Divorce, widowhood, remarriage and step-parenting are no less a meeting place than any other, a place where he can bind the wounds, heal the hurts, solve the problems and set the captives free.

Salvation, the acceptance of Jesus as Saviour and Lord is a real and attractive solution to those whose lives are messed up. To discover that you can't make a go of it yourself is one of the prerequisites of becoming a Christian. Only as we recognise the absolute futility of our own attempts to run things are we in a position to know our need of Jesus. Our human endeavour acts as a barrier, as impregnable as any portcullis. Laid down, it becomes the drawbridge for the Lord to walk upon, through which to enter our lives and take control, making sense out of the mess.

The blueprints for building

For the unbeliever and believer alike, all whose lives have been devastated by divorce or widowhood, there is tenderness and healing. For those struggling blindly in the throes of step-parenting, indeed for all who feel they have made a mess of things and can see no clear way forward, there is help and hope, with clear guidelines for the future. That hope, that healing and guidance—all that is needed in whatever situation—is to be found in the Bible, the history of God's relationship with mankind and his word to the people of today, and in a personal, daily relationship with the Lord.

A second marriage may be used by God to teach old lessons in a new way. Stepfamily relationships can be used similarly. Time and again, in the early months after our wedding, Paul and I remarked upon the feeling of going 'twice around the mountain'.[5] Just as the children of Israel were called out of bondage in Egypt, so too had we been taken out of similar situations—imprisoned by our own past, bound by the hurts and experiences inflicted upon us.

And like the children of Israel, we had often been slow to learn; stupid when it came to hearing the guidance of God, even rebellious. With gentleness and patience, we, like them, were taken over the same ground until the Teacher was satisfied with our progress.

Like Penny and Maurice, Barrie and Margot and dozens of other couples contemplating a second marriage for whatever reason, Paul and I embarked upon our new role as the parents of a stepfamily with little real knowledge of what lay ahead. We shared only a living, praying faith, and a great desire to succeed. One other quality seemed indispensable in the early years—an insatiable need to talk, to analyse, to question 'why'? To look back and learn from our mistakes, painful though it was, seemed often the only way forward in the search to discover the 'how' in building together the diverse components of individual personalities, to form one strong, united and meaningful family home.

Notes

[1] James 4:12
[2] Romans 8:28
[3] Malachi 2:16
[4] Joel 2:25

[5] The story of the children of Israel's wandering in the wilderness around Mount Horeb is found in Exodus and in Deuteronomy 1 comes the command to leave the area and move on.

2

Preparing the Ground

'Don't look now, but that's Felicity.'

In response to Lisa's hushed and conspiratorial tones, Penny glanced across the crowded little bistro where she and her friend were lunching. On the far side of the room a well-built woman of rather Bohemian appearance was easing her way into a window seat.

'Felicity?' Penny mouthed, raising an eyebrow enquiringly.

Lisa's head moved closer, her neatly cropped cap of hair shining under the restaurant's spotlights. 'The girls' mother,' she enunciated quietly.

'The girls' mother?' Incredulously, Penny repeated her words. 'You mean George's ex-wife?'

It scarcely seemed possible. Lisa and George seemed to match so well: both smartly dressed, intelligent people who, it had to be said, in spite of a good sense of humour, had a slight air of formality about them. Felicity, with her long straggling grey plaits and loose-flowing Indian-cotton garb just didn't seem to fit the picture.

Of course, it was some years since Felicity had walked out on George, and it could be that they had both changed. Or had an underlying incompatibility been the root cause of their marital breakdown? Whatever, there was certainly no doubting the fact that George was deliriously happy since his recent marriage to Lisa. But what intrigued Penny more than anything was not the suitability or otherwise of George's first wife, but how he coped with her presence in the same town in which he and his second wife now lived.

'He must have received a tremendous healing of the emotions,' she thought, remembering the pain of her own wounds. George, in common with most men, shared little in the way of feelings, even within the confines of their housegroup, but Penny knew from snippets which Lisa had let drop that he'd felt as hurt and rejected as anyone in the same situation, and had, in fact, fled abroad.

Demolishing dangerous structures

I could identify with that need to go quietly away and lick one's wounds. There had been several stages in my own experience, once my first marriage had come to an end, and in hindsight I could see how necessary each step had been in the process of preparing the ground before a further relationship could be successfully built.

My divorce, and all that had led up to it, had left me feeling as if I'd been torn in two. In retrospect that seemed a good analogy, since the Bible speaks of marriage as two people being merged into 'one flesh'. The pain and anguish of that 'one flesh' being torn limb from limb, so to speak, has to be experienced to be fully understood. Mercifully, nature's own anaesthesia seemed to take over for a while, bringing a numbing relief of sorts.

Then there was the guilt to contend with, the underlying feeling, 'Had I been a better husband/wife, would my marriage have succeeded?' Failure too, looms large in the mind of the divorcee, colouring every attitude, action and ideal. But perhaps worst of all were the feelings of rejection; the loss of self-esteem, amounting, sometimes, almost to a sense of utter worthlessness.

For me, it had been as if all the debris of that first marriage had to be cleared away, and it had proved to be something which could not be rushed. Bits of the old structure had remained standing: unrealistic expectations, false hopes, old habits, all of which had to be demolished.

Those parts which had suffered most damage during the onslaught of the broken relationship had been shored up with hurt pride, self-pity, suspicion. In some cases, so good was the barricade it had not only withstood the ultimate destruction—the divorce—but had actually been strengthened by it. But like all barricaded ruins, had it not been demolished along with the rest, it would effectively have prevented the successful building of any new relationship.

Perhaps it is this more than anything—the lack of awareness of the need for healing—that is most instrumental in putting strain on future relationships. The percentage of broken second, and even third marriages in the world would certainly seem to confirm this notion.

In Britain, we eschew the psychiatric counselling embraced by our American cousins, and have by and large an underlying contempt for what we see as their 'emotionalism'. Yet it is only in examining the emotions and subconscious dictates of our hearts that we can learn the lessons of past experience.

For the Christian there is yet more. We have at our disposal not simply the resources of a human agent, but the discernment of the Holy Spirit. In many instances I simply asked the Holy Spirit to show me those areas in which I needed healing and found, in my dreaming, or in quiet moments of the day, that hurtful experiences of the past, long since forgotten, were dredged up into my remembrance. For others the services of a skilled counsellor may be necessary to bring to the surface those deepest angers and hurts. But they also can call upon the spiritual gifts of wisdom, discernment and knowledge.

Nor, for the Christian, is it simply a matter of recognising and acknowledging those deepest wounds. This is where psychiatry leaves the job unfinished and, indeed, may often leave the patient with more 'hang-ups' than he started with. But in God we have the Divine Interior Designer. He who created my inmost being, who perceives my thoughts from afar and is familiar with all my ways, he who has ordained all my days and leads me in the way everlasting,[1] he alone can best set about the job of restoration. He alone knows what best to discard, what to salvage for the future. Anointed by God, the Lord has been sent, lovingly, into the world, to bind up the broken-hearted, to comfort all who mourn, and to anoint them in turn with the oil of gladness.[2]

Recognising my need early on, I'd responded to every book which the Lord had brought my way on the subject of emotional restoration, healing of the memories, healing of the mind. Like the woman who sought physical healing from the issue of blood, I'd reached out to touch the hem of the Lord's robe.[3] Following the example of the two blind men, I'd called upon the Lord, seeking healing.[4] Sometimes I'd had to ask forgiveness for my feelings towards the person who had wronged me, at others it was a matter of prayerfully forgiving them for the hurts they had inflicted upon me.

At times it was not as simple as that. I found, for instance, that though I loved them deeply, I bore a subconscious grudge against my parents, not for any hurt they had inflicted upon me, but for their passive influences in my life. Had the perfectionism I'd inherited from my father been instrumental in the breakdown of my marriage? Or was my mother's unbounding energy and unspoken contempt for inactivity responsible for the constant guilt I felt when it came to relaxation?

It was easy to forgive them because I loved them and because the standards they had instilled into me were intrinsically good; nor had they meant me any harm, but like all loving parents were interested only in my well-being. But nevertheless, my handling of these qualities in my life was at fault, as were my attitudes towards them. I had to ask God's forgiveness, consciously forgive my parents, and ask that these areas of perfectionism and guilt be brought under the control of the Holy Spirit.

During the six years of living alone, I'd sought counselling too. Gently, supportively, I'd been made to face the facts, grappling with my fears—both real and imaginary. Slowly, surely, I'd come to terms with those fears—of being unloved and unlovable, of my own inadequacies, of facing the future as a single parent.

As weeks gave way to months, I'd been brought up from the depths of the miry pit, where all is black and not even the feeblest illumination can penetrate to bring the smallest measure of understanding, or even acceptance of the situation. And I'd stood, at last, warmed by the gentle breezes brought by repentance, forgiveness, and dependence on God, beneath the light of the Son whose rays are pure, unadulterated Love. I'd known wholeness.

Or so I thought! And meeting Paul had seemed to be the culmination of that healing and wholeness. Basking in his love as our relationship developed, I'd longed for him to make me his wife.

'Where have you been all my life?' he would ask, gazing at me fondly. 'If we got married...' here would follow some tentative query as to my views on some matter or other, or perhaps a statement of intent on his part, or inquiry into practical issues. Heart beating faster, my hopes would be raised, only to be dashed moments later.

'But I'm not asking you...' he'd finish hastily.

The fact was, that though unknown to me at the time, he too had a past with which to come to terms, though the wounds in his experience owed nothing to a broken love affair but were the wounds of childhood.

Having talked all round the houses for months on end, my frustration knew no bounds. Would he never ask, I wondered? Finally, when presumably he felt he had received satisfactory replies to all his queries, Paul proposed one evening at his house. The magic moment had arrived, that moment for which I'd yearned so long.

'I'm not sure it's such a good idea,' I found myself replying stiffly. 'I'll have to think about it.'

It seemed inconceivable that I should react so negatively. Yet over the next few evenings, I voiced reason after reason why we should not marry. 'I'm older than you...' (less than four years separated us), 'our attitudes are so different in many ways...' (we had so much in common), 'our backgrounds are poles apart...' (yet our aims were so similar).

Blinded to all that had been good between us, I systematically set about pulling our relationship to pieces, raising 'issues' which were not issues at all, some of which are too shameful to recount.

For six weeks Paul endured my tirade, bewildered and hurt, yet waiting quietly and patiently for the tide to turn. Sometimes it seemed that the broader his shoulders, the more mightily I would wield the lash. It was almost as if I were testing the extent of his love. Or was I simply trying to destroy something which I could not handle, something which I feared might ultimately destroy me?

I even wrote to trusted friends—though only those who had never met Paul—couching the problem in such terms as to invite only their agreement with my sentiments. Sympathetically, they wrote back, endorsing my arguments.

Only my mother, sensing that all was not well between us, endeavoured to reason with me. Gradually, during one long lazy afternoon, as she spoke of the concern felt by my father and herself and frankly admitted that they had hoped to see me happily remarried, I began to see sense.

Hearing her put into words all that had attracted me to Paul, and the potential of a shared relationship, did much to help me regain my perspective.

For days, perhaps a week or more, I turned our conversation over and over in my mind, asking God to guide me. Eventually, in obedience to a growing conviction that I was to trust the Lord and that all the reasons I had advanced as to why we should not marry were without foundation or significance, I telephoned Paul.

'Do you still want us to get married?' I asked.

With some hesitancy, he agreed that he did, though he later admitted that he'd nearly given up hope.

But with an engagement ring on my finger and a date set for the wedding, there was still no improvement. Finally it all came to a head one evening when Paul telephoned me as usual.

'I've waited all these years to find the girl I want to marry,' he said, 'and I should be the happiest man alive.' A lump came into my throat in anticipation of what was to come. 'But I'm not,' he continued at the other end of the line. 'I just feel thoroughly miserable.'

It was more than I could bear. I hated myself for what I was doing to him, for what I was doing to us, and I knew I needed help.

Clearing the debris

Once again I sought the help of others, and through caring friends, and a ministry of deliverance, was counselled to wholeness and led to see that it was the reality of committing myself to a relationship akin to one which had caused me such unhappiness in the past, that was causing me to behave in such a way.

The love I felt for Paul was real enough, and as long as it had required no commitment had presented no threat.

Yet from the moment of his proposal that love had represented a risk; more than that, a dark foreboding of something already experienced. Fear of going back into the sort of union which had proved so unhappy in the past had provoked an involuntary fight within me, in an effort to put to death the whole relationship. With love killed between us, I would thus be saved from being 'sucked' by my emotions into something which my head reminded me was an undesirable state.

But more than that, I discovered also that in lashing out at Paul I was venting upon him all the pent-up emotion of the past — the hurt, frustration, anger and humiliation which had been invoked in me through my first marriage. This was a surprise. I had believed myself to be healed in this respect, especially since I had certainly come before the Lord and forgiven my 'ex', as well as asking God's forgiveness for my part.

'Sometimes,' my mentor explained to me, during one of my weekly counselling sessions, 'when hurts have gone very deep and piled up over a long period of time, though God does indeed bring a measure of healing, the operation has to be repeated.'

'So the healing I received in the past was real enough, but not deep enough?' I asked.

'That's right,' he replied encouragingly. 'If you think of a surgeon operating on a cancer victim whose disease is rampant and of considerable duration, you can probably understand that the treatment would almost certainly kill the patient if all the tumours were eradicated at once.

'It's much kinder and safer,' he continued as I nodded slowly, 'to perform several operations, giving the patient time to recover his strength in between.'

It made sense, as did also, his further counsel the following week. 'Though the institution of marriage which you are about to go into, is the same as the last time,' he began, once I had settled myself comfortably at one end of the settee and we had dispensed with the preliminaries, 'the actual relationship is entirely new and fresh.'

He paused long enough to see that I was following his line of reason, then continued. 'For one thing, Paul is a Christian, whereas your last husband was not. But as well as that, he is an entirely different person and your responses to him, your actions and interactions, can be made quite spontaneously. When we pray for your healing the Lord will wipe the slate clean for you to start again.'

Gradually, with these new insights, and the prayers of my counsellor, I learned how to entrust myself to the concept of a new commitment. Little by little, the realisation that this was to be a whole new, purpose-built second home, rather than a conversion job or patched-up, hand-me-down version of the first, filtered into my subconscious. With this came (but oh! so slowly) the sought-after change in my behaviour. And second-time-round was not to mean second-best!

Dealing with deficiencies in designing

As the leaders of a Christian singles' group, Paul and I had often commented privately upon the need of some of our members to find wholeness within themselves, prior to seeking a partner in life.

'It's sad really,' Paul would say. 'You see so many lonely, socially inadequate folk going round looking for someone to join forces with, when really they've little to offer.'

'Mmm,' I'd agree, 'they're like two halves trying to make a whole, but more often than not, it's the same half that's deficient in both—the same loneliness, the same inadequacies.'

'That's right!' Paul replied. 'You've got to be whole yourself, whether you're single, divorced or widowed. When I got to my late twenties and folk stopped asking me

"Are you married?" and started asking how many children I had, assuming that at my age I must be married, I realised it might never come my way, and that I had to get my life together anyway.

'So I started looking at other ways to meet my needs of companionship, like joining tennis and badminton clubs.' He paused for a moment, lost in thought. 'And of course you don't have to be married to have a home. I found buying my own house and doing it up really fulfilling.'

'That's exactly what I told Moya last week,' I said enthusiastically, referring to a young woman who had come to me for counselling. 'She says she's always having rows with her mother, is bored and frustrated and feels God has a down on her because he hasn't produced a husband for her.'

'Yes, it's easy to feel like that,' Paul replied. 'But you just have to get on with life and not allow self-pity to take over.'

I'd said just that to Moya, pointing out that as long as she went on living at home and depending on her mother for everything, she wasn't fulfilling any of the potential God created in her and was therefore only half a person.

'We're all made in God's image and have the characteristics of his creativity,' I'd explained gently. 'And you don't have to have a husband to fulfil your nest-building instincts. You'd find life so much more satisfying if you were using your gifts, and you'd be a more interesting person. Think of the fun you could have decorating your own home, perhaps even creating a tiny garden in a window box, experimenting with cooking, having friends in...'

All in all, Paul and I had had a good deal to say regarding wholeness. We both knew that it was more than simply being well-rounded socially; there was a spiritual dimension to wholeness which equated with knowing who you are in Christ, and having some idea of his purpose in your life.

The trauma I'd experienced around the time of our engagement had made me question whether, in fact, I was sufficiently 'whole' myself to be contemplating marriage. Even with all I'd discovered regarding the violence of my reactions to Paul, was I foolish to believe that I could succeed in an area where I knew myself to have failed previously?

Over the weeks leading up to our wedding I learned, from my counsellor, that being whole did not mean that all the i's would be dotted and all the t's crossed. Being whole is quite different to being perfect. We can be whole now, whereas we cannot be perfect in this life, though we are being made perfect.

A baby is a whole person, though very imperfect in its ability to function according to its full potential. The ability to speak, to walk, to have control of bladder and bowel are only slowly acquired. Dexterity, and the skills of reason evolve even more painfully and laboriously. Nor, even when we reach adulthood do we use a fraction of our physical and mental faculties, as any scientist would tell you. Though athletes strive toward physical perfection, no one seriously believes it to be attainable in this life.

The same is true of spiritual perfection. Though we are being transformed into the likeness of Jesus who is perfect, this is an ongoing process.

Wholeness, however, is dependent upon our bringing ourselves 'as a little child' to the Lord, just as we are, within the limits of our understanding of ourselves. In my weakness his strength is made perfect[5], and he is my all in all. Weighed in the balance, the deficiency of my spirit is compensated for by the provision of his Spirit. I am thus complete.

I remember the sheer magnitude of God's Word on this subject quite overwhelmed me the first time it sunk in, and continues to do so to this day. Colossians 2:9 and 10 says: 'For in Christ all the fullness of the Deity lives in bodily form, and you have been given fullness in Christ, who is the head over every power and authority.' In the Authorised Version, verse 10 is rendered: 'And ye are complete in him...' I am complete, not because of anything I do, but because all the fullness of the Deity dwells in me—nothing lacking.

I may thus be healed (and therefore whole) of all that the Holy Spirit has revealed to me of myself in the past and present, even though there will certainly be imperfections yet to be revealed in the future. This healing is like wiping the slate clean, or to bring the analogy more up to date, will have the effect of erasing all previous computer programming in my life. My actions and reactions, though they may still be imperfect for other reasons, will not, therefore, be dictated by what has gone before.

Keeping the site tidy

Trusting God, and being obedient to his leading, was what had brought Paul and me together after my initial outburst. Trusting him for the future was to continue to be part of the healing process. It was in the daily living out of our lives, an ever constant awareness of the need to continue and improve our communication skills, and above all, a willingness to humble ourselves 'for the Lord's sake', that this was to be accomplished.

For Paul himself, despite an ongoing process of healing brought about by our endless talking, analysing and praying together, one major area of healing did not take place until some three or four years after we had been married.

Provoked by some irrational behaviour on his part, I'd been stung into naming what I saw as his problem—a relic of childhood. Great was my surprise when, after due consideration, he agreed, telling me I had 'hit the nail on the head'. A private consultation with one of our elders, who had known him as a youngster, soon brought the relief which only God can grant. It was a problem which was never again to plague us.

With the major problems in my own life (as far as I knew them) now dealt with prior to our marriage, I was still to have niggling, petty issues erupting for some months after.

Counsellors and psychiatrists speak of 'no-go areas'. These are the experiences of past relationships which prove too painful to allow them to surface. As soon as a new relationship threatens by coming too close to the source of pain, we either back off or blow up.

Two personal experiences epitomised this issue for me in the early days of our marriage. One was the story of the white dress. It was a simple cotton dress which I'd made a year or two previously and which was a firm favourite. I'd donned it one warm summer evening and stood critically before the bedroom mirror.

'I'm not sure this suits me anymore now I've put on a bit of weight,' I said, turning this way and that. 'What do you think Paul?'

Whatever Paul thought was well concealed in one of those non-committal mumbles so well-loved of husband in this position.

'Don't you think it makes the tops of my arms look a bit fat?' I persevered. 'Perhaps I'm getting too old to wear sleeveless dresses?'

Now what I really wanted was reassurance—on two counts: one, that my favourite dress still suited me and made me look attractive, and two, that I was getting neither too old nor too fat to wear it! And I wanted the right answer no matter what!

Brought up to speak the truth always, and unused to the vagaries of women's vanity, Paul took prudence to be the better part of valour and agreed with me! It was like a red rag to a bull. Under normal circumstances such 'male foolishness' might have been dismissed with disdain. To a bride of a few weeks, with a broken marriage behind her and all the package of rejection and low self-esteem that that represents, it was anathema.

Once the tears and tantrums had died down, I was able to put on my 'counselling hat' and quite objectively explain to Paul the reasons for the tirade, and what was expected of him in order to avoid it in the future.

But to leave it as his responsibility in perpetuity would not only have been most unfair, but also a recipe for disaster. It is the way of the world to expect all our needs to be met in and by our partner, and it behoves Christians to realise that this can never be so. What I needed, and eventually sought in my private prayer time with the Lord, was the healing of those memories which triggered such irrational behaviour.

The second example which springs to mind was a few months on in our marriage. We were sitting companionably early one evening, preparing a bumper crop of apples for the freezer. Numerous telephone calls had interrupted our task, all from people whom I had been counselling. To be perfectly honest, much as I longed to lead these folk to wholeness, I was finding the intrusion upon time spent with my new husband rather irksome. I also felt a little tired and drained, in need of relaxation and refreshment with the one I loved.

Since Paul had answered the 'phone on each occasion and passed it on to me, he was obviously instrumental in the interruption. Vague, unexpressed feelings of wishing he would be more protective of our time together and my need of relaxation began to surface in me, in the form of a mild irritability, though whether this was directed toward Paul or the callers I am not sure.

Responding to one or two remarks I passed, and perceiving my tension, Paul stood behind me massaging my neck. 'You'll have to learn to say "no" sometimes,' he said mildly, 'or we'll never get any time together. And I do want to see something of my wife.'

Far from soothing me, I bristled inwardly. The balm I'd yearned for—that of my husband protecting and caring for me, his wife—I now perceived as a cloying, self-seeking male chauvinism which wanted to ensure that the 'little wife was always available to meet her husband's every need'. It was one of my no-go areas! Past experience having taught me that my life was always to be subordinate (and therefore dispensable) to my husband's, I now felt threatened. He was trying to stifle me!

The hurts and insecurities of the past lurk beneath the surface, as these had, ready to erupt (and this is the important bit) at what is seen to be threatening behaviour from the new partner, regardless of his or her actual motivation. Recognising this, talking it out together and asking each other's forgiveness, coupled with the 'reprogramming' of a new and loving relationship can, in themselves, bring a measure of healing. But in a sense this is only skin-deep.

Truly deep and effective healing is available only through Jesus. And this is effected only when we ask. To our knowledge, Jesus healed no one without their having desired it. And on each occasion when he asked 'Do you want to be healed?', a change in the behaviour and circumstances of life had to be faced.

Change is uncomfortable, often painful! For those who were healed in Biblical days there were major adjustments to be made. Blind beggars had to be prepared to work for their living. The lame had to learn to walk alone without the support of others. Sympathy for the sick would no longer be pertinent and responsibility for self and family would have to take its place.

The same is true of emotional wounds. We can become comfortable in our sense of self-pity, feeling our irrational behaviour to be justifiable because of our past. Behaviour patterns learned from those who have inflicted them upon us, can themselves be turned round, for us to inflict on our new partner. And this form of 'revenge' may be a source of relief to which we cling. If we truly seek healing, we have to be willing to let go, willing to change, willing to be made uncomfortable.

Before healing of the mind, the emotions and the memories can be effected, repentance may be necessary, a willingness to admit that you're wrong, a desire to turn to a new direction. And that is the greatest change of all. A change that is only attainable in the Lord.

Notes

1 From Psalm 139
2 From Isaiah 61
3 Matthew 9:20
4 Matthew 20:30
5 1 Corinthians 12:9

3

Family Foundations

The early evening sun was slanting in through the kitchen windows as Penny stood at the sink peeling potatoes. Glancing off the triangle of grass on the corner of the road, it had the mellow quality of autumn. A new term had begun—the first of her married life.

Penny's fears for how Maurice would cope with the increased commuting at the end of a day's teaching had been unfounded. The hour-long journey through beautiful countryside, though tiring in the early morning, had proved a buffer in the evenings, enabling him to shake off the fatigue of work and greet his new family refreshed and renewed. Even so, he was looking forward to when Penny's house would be sold and they could buy a home together in his hometown.

Hearing his key grating in the lock Penny dried her hands and made for the hall, leaving the potato peelings in the sink. Almost simultaneously she could hear Melony's footsteps flying down the stairs. It was the same every evening: a race to greet the man of the house—and her daughter won hands down.

By the time Penny arrived on the scene Mel was busy engaging Maurice in her usual sport, leaping at him from the half-landing, demanding piggy-back rides, or 'walking' on his feet like any seven or eight-year-old. The fact that she was thirteen seemed not to matter one jot. Good naturedly, Maurice would humour her childish claims upon his attention whilst, delighted with this developing relationship, Penny awaited her turn.

They had been married only a few months, yet once over her initial shyness with her new stepfather, Melony seemed to feel that he was her personal playmate. Sometimes, when the meal was cleared away and homework done, the romping and horseplay would continue later in the evening. Challenged by her interest in gymnastics, Maurice would become a climbing frame for her balancing acts, or, sitting crossed leg on the floor with her, contort his body into ever-more alarming shapes. When it came to attempting to push one leg behind his head, egged on and physically aided by this newly-energised daughter as she heaved at his foot, Penny drew the line. Visions of him lying in bed for months on end with a slipped disc were not exactly her ideal for early married life.

It amazed them both that this previously shy, awkward and thoroughly introverted teenager should so regress into the behaviour of a youngster. For years after her father had left and remarried, she had become increasingly more solemn—an old head on young shoulders. A general air of sadness and reserve seemed to have taken her over so that even her bodily movements had seemed inhibited. Thankfully, since Penny's marriage to Maurice, that seemed to be in the process of changing.

Having been a step-child himself after his mother's death and father's remarriage, Maurice had been well aware of the problems they might have encountered. He understood too, the emotions aroused in a child upon hearing that the remaining parent is to be remarried, and had expressed his concern early on in a letter.

'...and there is Melony to consider,' he had written some weeks after marriage had become a serious proposition in his relationship with Penny. 'I could marry you tomorrow and we know that we could work at it and be extremely happy and content.

'However,' the letter continued, 'I don't believe that you have given her enough thought—at least, if you have, you haven't really said so. Put yourself in her place—suddenly having to uproot, not necessarily housewise, but certainly relationshipwise, and having, suddenly, to live with a relatively strange man.'

'I think, having now been married to him for some years,' Penny laughingly told me, 'he meant to imply that he was a relative stranger, rather than that there was anything odd about him as a person!'

'But he was right,' she admitted. 'At least in so far as the fact that Maurice and Mel had been like strangers. There had been so little opportunity for them to get to know one another, since Mel was, at that time, a weekly boarder at school.

'But far from giving her no thought, I'd been very sensitive to her feelings, especially at weekends, when I knew she would want me to herself.'

Penny had pondered long and hard on all that Maurice had written, before reading on: 'She is an emerging adolescent, already revealing itself in her conversation with you, even in front of me. Just imagine that she and I didn't get on. That would break your heart, and probably our relationship.... Imagine the strain that could have on us, and Melony would sense it too. Darling, these are my real fears for us.... I must get to know Melony, not just as a friend of her mum's....

'Do you want us to be an instant family, or mother and daughter and man and wife? What does Melony want? She can't really be expected to answer that yet as she doesn't know me sufficiently well, but that question must be answered ultimately, darling...our situation demands more than the normal responses between two people...'.

'More than the normal responses between two people...' He'd been right there, Penny thought. A second marriage was far more complicated than a first. There were so many people to consider.

And so, prior to their marriage, they'd discussed at length the implications for Penny's daughters. Not that it would really affect the older one, she had already left home. Was she being selfish in wanting to marry Maurice, Penny had wondered? Were her motives pure?

'I don't think there's any advantage in her having to grow up in a one-parent family,' she'd told Maurice frankly. 'She's seen the bad side of the coin, a marriage that failed and parents that fought. Now I want her to see that it can work, that man and wife can live together in love and harmony and peace.'

Agreeing that that made sense, Maurice felt, nevertheless, that more time was needed for he and Melony to get to know one another. 'It's a tremendous adjustment all round,' he mused, recollecting his own experiences, 'especially if you've had any length of time, as she has, to get used to having one parent to yourself. I wouldn't want her to resent me, to feel that I was breaking up the special, close relationship she has with you.'

Much time was spent in prayer, not only that Melony could accept Maurice happily, but also that he and Penny would continually be sensitive to her feelings and have the wisdom to know how to handle them. The problem of finding time for the two to get to know one another better had eventually been solved when, as a result of the cessation of maintenance and school fees from her father, Melony had come home to live, attending the local grammar school. Gradually, though still very shy, she had come to accept Maurice and a relationship of sorts had been established. Watching her romping with him now, it seemed to Penny that their prudence had paid off.

Digging deep

In our own situation, Paul's past experience had given us a heightened awareness of the problems peculiar to us as a potential stepfamily. Nevertheless, we were aware, too, that our own situation was relatively simple. Numerically, because of my daughter's absence from home, there were few of us involved in the meshing together of different members of the family.

I had often thought, during my years as a divorcee, that if ever I were to be blessed with a second marriage, it would have to be with someone in a similar position—namely a divorced man with a family of his own. In that way, I had reasoned, he would be used to children.

Subsequent to my marriage to Paul, however, my observation of the plight of others had caused me to reconsider. Though my friend Lisa had obviously been well endowed with grace to cope with George's ex-wife and his two teenaged children living in close proximity, I was glad now, that I had not had this added complication to face. But God gives grace where it is needed, and we had an equal abundance to call upon to fit our own set of circumstances.

As Christians we had had the benefit of prayer and the guidance of the Holy Spirit. With discernment and sensitivity we had been able to draw upon Paul's past experience of the situation. A building is only as secure as its foundations are solid. When it came to building our relationships, we had a wealth of funds to draw upon: a foundation dug deep into the love of Jesus, set firm in the Word of God and bonded together with prayer and love.

But not all families are so rich in their resources and it is small wonder that second and subsequent marriages so often fail. A recent television documentary highlighted the way in which infatuation for each other can blind a couple to the well-being of their children.

Only weeks after beginning a relationship, mum's boy-friend moved into her home, in the role of stepdad to her two daughters. With virtually no time for the thirteen-year-old and fifteen-year-old to get to know him it was hardly surprising when they showed little respect for either him or their mother, both of whom had shown such a complete lack of sensitivity towards their feelings.

To compound matters still further, the stepfather's young son and daughter then moved in. This resulted in the three girls (mother's two and father's one) having to share a room. The boy was relegated to the landing! An inconvenience not only to him but to the whole family.

It was enough to make you weep to see the hostility between the youngsters, two of whom obviously felt completely threatened by the sudden invasion of their home, whilst the younger two, who with their father were cast in the role of invaders, struggled bravely to put on a good face and were stoutly defensive of their own position.

Needless to say, such intolerable living conditions eventually saw the virtual destruction of the stepfamily. One couldn't help but feel like shaking them when the couple, who continued to see one another after stepdad and family had moved out once more, remarked naively, 'We could have made it on our own' or words to that effect.

* * * * * *

Two of the most successful step-families we have observed for ourselves are those of Simon and Ros and of Isobel and Warren. In both cases, whether intentionally or not, there was a considerable length of time prior to the marriages taking place, for relationships to be established between the prospective step-parent and children.

In Ros' and Simon's situation this had come about more through expediency rather than any planning on their part, when his second wife had walked out of the home leaving him to take care of the two little ones. A non-Christian, and with two failed marriages now behind him, he was not in a hurry to embark upon a third. But a developing romance with Ros, and her naturally affectionate and caring disposition made her, eventually, the ideal person to take over mothering the two toddlers when Simon's mother was unable to continue with the task. By the time Ros moved in, the children knew and trusted her.

'I moved in to see if I could accept the two little ones as my own children,' Ros smiled. Just seeing her with them was proof enough that she'd succeeded in doing so.

After two years of living together, it was Simon's conversion which brought the intimacy of their relationship to an end rather than any lack of compatibility. And by the time Ros too had made a commitment to the Lord and she and Simon were joined in marriage, a firm trust and loving affinity had grown up between them all. The children had had time to adjust. They had become a family.

Isobel's situation was similar in that, with a college course to complete, she was in no hurry to marry Warren when they met soon after her divorce.

'Really, it was the children who proposed to him,' she told us with a wry smile. 'There had been a couple of years when I was the only one on the scene after their father left, and both girls wanted to be a family again. When Warren came along, they kept asking if he was going to be their new daddy. Every time Claire got a new pair of shoes she kept asking, "Are these my bridesmaid's shoes?" '

Warren laughed uproariously in agreement: 'They saw a lot of me when I returned from abroad,' he said. 'I wasn't working for a while so I used to do odd jobs around the house for Isobel.'

'Yes,' Isobel interrupted. 'I was at college and had an au pair to look after the girls, so it meant they built up a relationship with Warren which didn't include me. In a way I was the odd one out,' she smiled warmly. 'Although at the time it seemed hard for Warren to be unemployed, I think the Lord must have arranged it so they could have an opportunity to get to know one another without me around.'

'So how did they take it when you eventually told them you were getting married?' I asked.

'Oh,' Isobel cried, 'their first question to Warren was, "Does that mean we can call you Daddy now?" '

'We had planned a holiday with them at a well-known Christian Conference Centre in Kent,' Warren took up the story once more. 'When we decided to get married without waiting for Isobel to finish her course, that became our honeymoon. We're the only couple I know who took the kids away on honeymoon!'

They both laughed. 'We hadn't the heart to let the girls down,' Isobel finished. 'We just exchanged Warren's single and our family room for two doubles.'

Setting firm footings

Even having allowed for a natural relationship to develop before thrusting the two families upon one another, the way in which children are told of the impending nuptials is all important. The application of a certain amount of psychology in this, as in many other areas of life, works wonders. I learned, as part of my Sunday School training, that attitudes can be infectious.

If you approach the matter negatively, with embarrassment, or in fear and trepidation, you place a weapon in the hands of the child. Being of 'fallen nature', as we all are, they are quickly aware of the fact that they hold the balance of power. A tentative 'would you like to do so and so,' opens up the possibility of a 'no' answer, whereas an enthusiastic 'let's do...' usually has the opposite effect.

'Look darling, I know it's not going to be easy for you, but X and I are thinking...that is...we'd like to...er...get married' is hardly going to win the support of your offspring, nor inspire them with enthusiasm. Such an approach offers them, on a plate, the right to decide the course of your life, inviting a negative response.

Seems silly, doesn't it? Yet it is amazing how many people, these days, adopt these attitudes with their children. I remember counselling a divorced woman who asked her youngsters if they would mind very much if they all moved across country to be nearer other family members, including her own mother, and was surprised and disappointed when they rebelled.

In my opinion, and I am aware that this runs counter to much of the 'progressive' approach advocated today, children are not equals from whom permission has to be sought, though this is not to say that they cannot be diplomatically sounded out. But too often we give them a share in the decision making, and far from being to their advantage, this places upon them onerous responsibilities which should not be theirs.

In these days, when we hear so much of 'rights' (and little of the responsibility which goes hand-in-glove with such rights), it is well to remember the God-given right of children—namely, their right to dependency. They need, and have a right to expect, parents who make decisions on their behalf.

We, as parents, are called upon to be as God in their lives; that is, we are to model ourselves on his example as a Heavenly Parent, neither fearing discipline[1], nor imposing our wills upon them so as to provoke them[2]. Our decisions should, therefore, be based upon sound judgement, and this is only arrived at when we have prayerfully weighed up the consequences of our proposed actions, and taken into consideration the well-being of our children. It's all a question of balance.

Even so, having chosen the right moment to break the news, and adopted the right attitude, care must be taken not to go to extremes. Telling a young child with great enthusiasm and gusto that 'We're having a new daddy' may smack of a supermarket acquisition. To youngsters brought up in an age of consumer expendability, this attitude may foster and condone the ideology of 'new is best'.

It is no coincidence that instant credit, plus immediate accessibility of mass produced goods, and their transient, 'biodegradable' nature has gone hand-in-glove with the eroding of *all* that is intended to be durable in life. The supply and demand for such instant acquisition spills over into our expectations of relationships, so that we embrace, also 'biodegradable' divorces, instant remarriage and ready-made second families.

In the days when a piece of furniture was hewn from mighty oaks which had stood for a hundred years, and which took months of patient craftsmanship and tender loving care to transform into a thing of beauty and useful- ness, and when a livelihood was rooted in the cyclical pattern of nature's seasons, then the whole basis of life, of relating to one another, of rearing one's family, was rooted in the same slow, rhythmical design. We, as Christians, have an awesome responsibility to future generations to counter the hectic nature of our present-day lifestyle which will lead, ultimately, to the destruction of society as we know it.

Yet divorce and remarriage are facts of life, and if a fact of your life, then a positive approach should be taken. Children, young and old, need simply to know that you view the intended addition to the family as beneficial to all, someone to be regarded as a gift from the Lord—a part of his bountiful provision and blessing.

These were the attitudes prevailing when Leslie broke the news of his impending marriage to his two teenage daughters.

'From the very beginning the sheer goodness of Laura

impressed them,' Leslie told me. 'No hint of jealousy from either of them over her. Indeed, they found it thrilling that they were going to their Dad's wedding.'

Barrie's and Margot's children, whose respective parents had gone off together, apportioned no blame, though Barrie and Margot privately each blamed the other's spouse for 'stealing' their own.

'The kids were over the moon when we told them we were going to be married,' Margot recalled. 'But they had had two years to get used to the idea.'

This was not the case, however, in Doreen and Jeff's experience. 'My youngest daughter, who was about sixteen at the time, really resented it when I said I was getting married,' Doreen told me ruefully. 'She was so rude when Jeff came to stay, I used to dread it. I thought I'd lose Jeff because of her.

'I remember one weekend when I took Jeff a cup of early morning tea—he slept in the spare room—I left the door open as usual, but Amy called something out, implying that we were having an affair.'

'Yes, it was dreadful,' Jeff confirmed. 'Nothing was further from the truth.'

'Anyway,' Doreen took up the story once more, 'one day my parents suggested I let her live with them, so she did. I'd always told the girls not to consider me if they wanted to move. I didn't want to hold them back.'

Subsequently, after a cooling off period, Amy told her mother that she couldn't bear the thought of her sleeping with another man after the death of her father. Her seemingly incomprehensible behaviour suddenly took on a new light.

'They'd lost their dad,' Doreen said understandingly. 'They'd been let down by another male member of the family, and I'd previously been involved with another man who said he wanted to marry me but was just using me to get custody of his child. They must have felt, "Oh,

no! We don't have to go through all that again!" Once
they realised that Jeff was genuine, it was OK.'

Doreen felt no need to play down the wedding arrangements, despite the aforegoing conflict, and as a widow was
married in church with long white dress, veil and all the
trimmings. One daughter from each family officiated as
bridesmaids.

Laura too, as a first-time bride, chose white, with
Leslie's daughters as bridesmaids.

'Laura's family were naturally a bit concerned at first,'
Leslie admitted, 'that she had met this divorced father of
two big daughters. But they quickly showed their love to
me and the girls.'

Though previously doubting his eligibility to be married in church, Leslie was relieved, for Laura's sake, to
discover that with two of his future brothers-in-law in
Holy Orders, this posed no obstacle.

For Barrie and Margot no such problem existed. 'As a
confirmed atheist at the time,' Margot told us, 'I had no
desire to marry in church before a God I didn't believe in.
So we married in a registry office—second time for me,
though Barrie had been married in church first time.'

A good deal of sensitivity needs to be combined with
communication when it comes to understanding the children's emotions. Doreen's daughter's aversion to her marriage had been rooted in loyalty to her deceased father.
Talking things through had resolved those feelings of
betrayal. Similar feelings may exist in different circumstances. Where older children have formed bonds of
friendship and closeness over a period of years with the
custodial parent, that parent's new alliance may seem
threatening, undermining the intimacy of the parent/child
relationship.

Although I firmly adhere to the concept of parents
being parents rather than friends to their children, inevitably bonds of parity will be formed with older offspring.

Paul, when he was only seventeen, had found a growing camaraderie between himself and his father during the months after his mother's death. A fraternity grew up between them, two men, living together, thrust into a companionship which obviously could not continue in the same way once his father remarried. A similar situation existed between my eldest daughter Susie and myself, though less so than in Paul's case, since she was, at the time of my marriage, living and working away from home.

Such ties need to be severed gently if jealousy and resentment are to be avoided between step-child and step-parent. More will be written of this in Chapter 5.

A certain amount of natural reserve and shyness in both Paul and me dictated the tenor of our wedding. Neither of us wanted a big affair, and though I did not want in any way to cheat Paul, whose first time it was, I felt very sensitive about my children. It seemed to me that to make too much of this second wedding was to make a further travesty of the vows made between their father and me. I had no desire to rub salt into the wound.

Nevertheless, despite our desire to play down the event, both Paul and I felt strongly that if our marriage was sanctified in God's eyes, as we believe it was, then we certainly wanted to be married in church. As committed Christians, to leave God out of the proceedings would have made a mockery of the whole union.

Anyone feeling likewise would be well advised to ask around. Most of the free churches are willing to judge each case on its merits; or if preferred, a blessing following a civil service is almost always available in the Church of England.

But weddings are more than the bringing together of two people. Just as Laura's parents and family had affirmed their acceptance of Leslie into the family, and pleasure in their marriage, so too did mine. The forty or so guests we had between us had been blessed with a superb buffet reception in what I fondly consider to be one of the most beautiful settings in England—my parents' garden.*

Cementing together—what's in a name?

What the children call their new step-parent will be largely dictated by their age and the type of relationship which exists between them prior to the marriage. But there is one other factor—the desire of the heart.

Mother's 'boyfriend', or Dad's 'girl' may pose no threat to the security of offspring initially, but with the advent of marriage between them, the existing relationship of 'friend', 'uncle', or 'auntie' may take on a whole new concept. Many little girls respond well to a new man in Mummy's life, even to the extent, where there has been deprivation in their own lives, of flirting quite unabashedly, as Isobel's did with Warren.

Paul finds in the classroom that many children from broken homes show their need of affection in the most overt manner, finding constant excuses for physical contact ranging from 'leaning' to openly climbing on his knee. Sadly, in the twisted society in which we live, this sort of behaviour has to be monitored carefully. Conversely, there are those whose family backgrounds are such as to cause them to shun all human touch; early in life they erect barriers to protect their vulnerability from further hurt.

Whilst many will welcome the advent of a new Daddy or Mummy, to others this will be salt in the wound, reinforcing the pain and anguish of the absent parent, whether this be by death or divorce. Sensitivity needs to be shown. If 'Daddy' is the man who takes them to the zoo on Sundays, then he cannot also be the man who has come

* More will be written of the grandparents' position in Chapter 10.

to live with Mummy. 'Pops', 'Pa', 'Dad' or 'Da' may be substitutes which are far more acceptable to young hearts and minds.

My own children were of an age where to call Paul 'Daddy' would have been unthinkable, not only to them but to him also! After years of bachelorhood, he admitted early on in our courtship how daunting he found the prospect of marrying a divorcee with teenage daughters.

'I would suddenly have to face the world, friends, colleagues, callers at the front door with "and this is my wife" (no problem) "and step-daughter" ', he wrote, going on to confess his inability of facing up to that situation at the time.

Since I had been a teenage mother, my eldest daughter was just twenty when Paul and I married. Parenthood is an evolving role, a gradual unfolding and growing into and cannot suddenly be thrust upon one. Though a good relationship exists between Susie and he, there was never any real possibility of its being filial/paternal. But that is not to say that it is just like any other relationship outside the family. Inevitably, family feelings of loyalty, pride, affection, protection and belonging have eventually blossomed from the soil of simple friendship and respect.

Paul has always been simply Paul to the girls, but away from home, Susie's desire is to be known as a 'normal' family, and she refers to us both as her 'parents'. Neither she nor the other two correct those who refer to Paul as 'Dad' or their 'father', nor does Paul correct those who refer to his 'daughters', though we make no effort to hide the fact that we are a stepfamily. It's simply a matter of economics and aesthesticism. 'Step...' takes longer to say and seems, somehow to demand the preposition 'wicked'. The concept has traditionally been made unattractive.

Sometimes the question of names and roles can cause conflicts of a different kind when viewed from another perspective. In families where there are children from both sides, it obviously makes for greater unity if all call each parent by the same name. For the child of one parent to be calling the step-parent by Christian name, whilst the other children address him/her as Mum or Dad can give rise to feelings of separateness, perhaps even isolation.

'I was always "Dad" to Margot's girls,' Barrie told us, 'but my eldest son always called Margot by her Christian name.'

'He seemed so grown up to me, compared to my own two,' Margot confessed, 'though I realise now he was only a little boy himself.

'But years later, when his sister wanted to call me by my Christian name when she was thirteen, I objected and wouldn't allow her. She had never really called me anything. Eventually, a friend asked her what she would really like to call me and she said "Mummy". I think she felt left out being the only girl not to call me Mummy.'

Feelings of disloyalty to her own mother had to be surmounted initially, but the term 'Mummy' now comes quite naturally to Zoe's lips.

Obviously, the younger the child, the easier the transition. But even with Isobel's children, who had been longing to adopt Warren as Daddy, the actual switch from Christian name to 'Dad' caused them some embarrassment and mirth, though they had their father's permission to do so. Strangely enough, it seems to cause them no problem giving the same title to both natural and step-parent and both 'Dads' seem to wield an authority and influence in the children's lives.

Simon's children too, found no problem in giving the same title to mother and stepmother.

'Kevin's wedding present to me was to call me Mum,' Ros explained. 'I started as Ros, then Mummy Ros. When we got married, he asked what he should call me and I said anything you like as long as it's not nasty. He said, I'll call you Mum then.'

'How did the children's mother take to them calling
you Mum?' I asked Ros.

'She's been very good.' Ros looked to Simon for confirmation.

He nodded. 'Give her her due, she's been no trouble.'

If only it were always that simple!

Notes

[1] Proverbs 3:11, 12
[2] Ephesians 6:4

4

Establishing an Equitable Economy

Dubiously Penny stood before the record counter in Woolworths then turned on her heel and made for the door, stopping abruptly and retracing her steps once more. The shop assistant eyed her with suspicion; Penny had been hesitating for some time, debating. Quickly, before she could change her mind yet again, she selected the album of love songs and paid for it.

It was an un-birthday present for Maurice; a celebration gift for the three-monthly anniversary of their marriage. Penny knew he would appreciate her choice, it was just that she was so unused to spending money so freely. Richard, her 'ex' had neglected to pay any maintenance during the last few years since their divorce, and there had been a spell on supplementary benefit. After years of not working whilst married, the only job Penny had been able to find had been poorly paid, and frivolous items like records were not on the shopping list. It was hard to feel free after all those years of restraint.

Not that she and Maurice had much to spare since their wedding. But Penny was glad, as she stepped into the High Street clutching her purchase, that she at least now had the option. She and Maurice had not gone into marriage in blind ignorance of each other's financial situation, but had been frank and open in their discussions.

It had been a warm day in late spring some months
after their engagement as the two of them had lain in the
garden. Above them the sky rose in a high dome of the
most intense blue, enhanced by the whiteness of tiny
cloud-tufts as they drifted slowly past. All around were the
busy sights and sounds of an activity with one aim in
mind, that of bringing to fruitfulness the abundance of
newly created life. Birds sang, bees buzzed, beetles scur-
ried. One could almost hear the plants themselves as they
strained upward and outward.

Sparkling on Penny's left hand was further evidence of
the fruits of the earth—the brilliance of a tiny chip of
carbon, surrounded by fiery pieces of corundum. The
diamond signified durability, the gold mount purity and
the rubies inestimable value, whilst the ring itself, a circle
without beginning or end, symbolised the eternal nature of
the love it conveyed.

To the casual observer it might have seemed very
romantic as the two lay face down, propped up on their
elbows in earnest conversation. But the fact of the matter
was that spread before them were pages and pages torn
from old exercise books, covered with scribbled figures.
With their wedding day now fixed, they were busily
engaged in discussions of the most pecuniary nature.

Some might feel it mercenary, perhaps even a little
mechanical, to be thinking of income and expenditure at
such a time. But far from debasing love the sharing of
one's financial pledge to the other is a measure of the
degree of commitment. For the fact is, it is upon financial
disunity that marriages often founder.

Financial footings

Money, and the material possession which it can procure,
represents one of our most basic forms of security. Even a
babe suckling at its mother's breast relies, indirectly, upon

her economic ability to feed herself in order that she in turn may nourish her offspring.

There has been a tendency amongst some Christians to look with contempt upon 'filthy lucre', seeing privation as a virtue. The implication is that money is somehow 'unspiritual'. But as someone once said, the ego can fatten itself as well on the pride of poverty as on the pride of wealth. It is not money itself which is the root of evil, but the love of money.[1] Of itself, it has no merit or dismerit, it is simply the evolution of bartering, the means by which we trade that which we have earned, for that of which we have need.

All too often, however, we despise the mention of money, whilst secretly elevating its significance to us. Publicly denying its importance in our lives, we nurse those feelings of fear (of lack), pride (in acquisition) or avarice (for accumulation).

The couple who are unable to be open in this respect are thus holding back in their mutual trust of one another. Complete honesty is needed, and that means making yourself vulnerable. If I, as a woman, for example, am to entrust myself to the provision of a man for my security, it surely behoves him to trust me sufficiently to let me know the extent to which he can provide? I might well be forgiven for taking any reluctance to do so on his part, as an indication of his lack of confidence in me.

Does he believe that if he divulges all, I might take advantage, sucking him dry in a lifetime of spend, spend, spend? Is his love of me such that he can give only partially, believing that he has an inherent right to the greater part for his private use? Is he afraid that he might be denied those pleasures to which he clings, and which are personal to him, unable to be shared with a spouse? Or is it that he believes my estimation of his worth as a person (and husband) rests in his bank balance and earning potential?

And if I continue to earn, does this undermine his self-esteem? Does his own self-image require a wife who is utterly dependent? And how, if she is not, does she view the income she earns? Is she one of those women who consider her money as hers and his as hers too—at least jointly?

Although these questions may not overtly form part of any discussion, the answers should be part of a fund of knowledge each partner has of the other. Unless mutual openness and trust are an established part of the relationship in this, as in all areas, can it really be considered a firm foundation on which to build a life together? And where there are already children from a previous marriage, it becomes even more essential to explore one another's commitment at this level.

Discussions need to include the factor of maintenance, where this is payable by the absent natural parent; the possible loss of income where one partner in the proposed second marriage has been in receipt of a widow's pension after the death of the first husband; and whether the new marriage will necessitate the wife having to find a job in order to make a contribution to the family's income.

Laying down the guidelines

Doreen, who remarried some years after the death of her first husband had to face the fact that in losing her widow's benefit, she was losing also a piece of her independence. A similar situation may arise for many divorced women, whose own maintenance would automatically cease upon remarriage.

For those fortunate enough to continue receiving maintenance from their former husband on behalf of the children, this represents some small measure of liberty, just as the payment of Child Benefit does. At very least it means that she does not have to ask for every last penny from her new husband, even down to buying him a birthday card.

Theoretically, the situation should be easier if the couple agree to have joint bank accounts. But even here a non-working wife may feel diffident about drawing upon what she sees as essentially her new husband's money, in order to feed, clothe or entertain her own children. And though he, theoretically, is quite prepared to take on responsibility for her offspring, the actuality of the arrangement may cause resentment; he may well find her call upon his finances in this respect rather more than he had bargained for.

One way round this is to formulate a budget. By working out exactly what expenses will be per month throughout the year, a fair division can be made. A list can then be drawn up of which bills will be solely the husband's responsibility, which the wife's. An amount can then be made available to her, payable either in cash, into a post office or building society account, or into a separate bank account.

In this way both parties know exactly where they stand regarding their own responsibilities, yet each has freedom to move within that structure. If little Johnny is having a birthday party at the end of the month, Mum is thus able to make allowance within her monthly budget, by cutting down on something else earlier on in the month rather than having to go 'cap-in-hand' to ask for a specific sum.

Since I had a small private income, as well as maintenance for one child when Paul and I married, rather than pool our resources and then have an allowance made available to me, we kept our incomes separate. Each area of expenditure was then itemised and divided between us in proportion to our individual means. For reasons which will be made clear in future chapters, we felt it desirable for Paul to take on responsibility for all those areas which were our most basic needs. These included shelter, food and warmth.

Adding together the annual mortgage repayments, life assurance, house insurance, rates, gas, electricity, telephone and food, we then divided the total by twelve and arrived at a monthly figure which could easily be covered by Paul's salary cheque.

The first three items are paid on standing order. The remainder he then withdraws every month from his bank account and pays into a building society account. In this way we are covered for every bill that comes in, be it monthly, quarterly or annually. In addition, we make a small amount of interest in the building society when money accumulates between bill payments. The alternative to this scheme, whereby monthly payments are made direct to the companies concerned, means that they make the interest!

My income then tops up the housekeeping monies (milk bill, newspapers etc), pays most of our car expenses, contents insurance, clothes us, pays the TV licence, and covers all Christmas expenses and other gifts throughout the year. We each tithe from our own incomes, though such decisions are taken jointly, as well as any extra giving. We then take joint responsibility for all other expenses—house and garden maintenance, holidays and entertainment—if we're fortunate enough to have anything left over!

In addition we both have small savings schemes (Paul's regular, mine spasmodic), so that in the event of an emergency (either ours or anyone else's) we are able to make provision. An annual review ensures an up-date on changing circumstances.

We are not alone in this method of budgeting, whereby an openness and honesty exists quite harmoniously with separate bank accounts. But there are marriages known to me where this sort of arrangement would be unthinkable.

Assuming that being the Head, as laid down in Ephesians[2] means that they should hold the purse strings so tightly their wives can have no inkling of what is available, some husbands would take our system as quite unscriptural. Paul, however, believes that as Head he has the right to delegate, and that in making me responsible for certain areas of expenditure, his Headship is not in anyway undermined.

This would also seem to be supported in Old Testament thinking, since the Good Wife of Proverbs fame[3] had jurisdiction over the entire domestic household, as well as wheeling and dealing in the odd vineyard or two, and running highly successful cottage industries in various lines. She, alone, considered how to invest her earnings, and her trading was profitable. She too, was responsible for distributing help to the poor and needy. 'Worth far more than rubies...' to her husband, she was a woman of noble character (v. 1), blessed and revered by her family (v. 28), respected and praised in the community.

Yet her husband's Headship was not in any way threatened by her capabilities. Living as they did, in a patriarchal society, he was still a respected member of the local council, taking his seat 'among the elders of the land'. He had, we are told, 'full confidence in her', lacking nothing. And because he was able to entrust to her certain responsibilities, he was freed to help in the governing and welfare of the community.

* * * * * *

Another system of management is the joint bank account, and this is the method adopted by Doreen and Jeff. We went to see them some eight or nine months after they were married and learned of their arrangements as we sat sipping coffee in their lounge.

'Jeff gives me the housekeeping in cash,' Doreen said

matter-of-factly. 'But if I want something extra I can have it, can't I?' A warm smile lit her eyes as she fondly regarded her husband. 'He knows I'm not extravagant. We have a joint personal account but I've never written a cheque. I'm very careful, so Jeff trusts me.'

Jeff nodded, returning her smile. 'Any profit from the business will be joint. We decided that eventually, when a surplus has built up in the business account, we'd take it out and put it to earn interest. What we haven't decided yet is whether Doreen should have half in her own name, or whether we'll have a joint Building Society Account.'

Doreen looked thoughtful. 'Yes. Originally, I would have liked for all our money to be pooled—right from the sale of our houses and all we had before we were married.' She paused, as if unsure of how well we would accept what she had to say. 'But now,' she continued, 'I feel I'd like to have something of my own in case something should happen to my girls. I'd like to feel I could get at it quickly in an emergency instead of waiting sixty days to get it out of the Building Society.'

Rising to pour more coffee, Doreen launched forth into her recent difficulties in trying to lay hands quickly on some of her own money to take away on holiday. 'I wanted to be able to buy presents for my family without having to use what I still consider is Jeff's,' she concluded. The raised eyebrows and shrugged shoulder as Doreen finished her tale, spoke volumes of the problems she is still encountering in trying to think of her new husband's money as her own.

Maintenance

Since Doreen's daughters were beyond the age of receiving Child Benefit, her choices were restricted. For the mothers of youngsters, the receipt of weekly payments on behalf of their children can represent a tiny life-line with which to ease them into the role of renewed dependence in the second marriage. But what of those who are in the reverse situation—the givers rather than receivers?

Cathy was single prior to her marriage. Her step-children were adult and therefore independent. Nevertheless, Cathy and Max had the burden of her own commitments to consider in their discussions on finance.

'I still make payments to my mother who lives overseas,' Cathy explained. 'Obviously, this remains my responsibility.'

Equally obviously, matters such as this must be disclosed so that the other partner has the opportunity to take it into consideration and so that both may approach the situation in an attitude of shared concern. Marriage is not simply the coming together of two people in isolation, but the bonding together of two whole families. Each partner should therefore be prepared to take on a degree of accountability toward the parents, offspring and relatives of the other.

Much has been written in recent years about the resentment felt by second wives towards the husband's first family and their call upon his income, effort and time. This is especially true if the second wife has to work, whilst the first wife stays at home with her children. Public opinion has at times been cruel in labelling the stay-at-home wife a 'parasite' and legislation has sought to lessen the extent of responsibility by the father. There are those who lobby for the abolition of maintenance from ex-partners, and feel that it should fall to the State to provide for one-parent families.

This, in fact, is often what happens, when a man pleads his inability to support two families. During the course of counselling, I have seen young mothers struggling to eke out a meagre existence on Supplementary Benefit whilst the second family seems to fare rather better. Although the reverse may also be true, at least the second wife has the emotional and practical support of a husband.

But it must be said that potential second wives have a right to know the true extent of financial involvement with the first family before committing themselves to the marriage. But having done so (or having been instrumental in the break-up of the first marriage) there is no justification for complaint.

Sometimes, however, in spite of putting a second wife fully in the picture, the reality of living out the situation may be much harder than was thought. Simon's second wife, Daphne, found it so, and felt a growing jealousy of his ex-wife.

'We were very poor at one stage,' Simon explained. 'The maintenance came first for me, and though she agreed in principle, the test comes in practice. I'd lost the house—my first wife needed it for the kids. We were all living in the same town and there was a lot of bad feeling between the two women, and all round.

'I missed the kids dreadfully. There she was living in a great big house and Daphne and I were in a grotty council house.'

Perhaps because of this, when Daphne walked out on Simon and their two children, a lump sum was made payable to her, rather than continuing maintenance. Simon had custody of the children from the second marriage in any case, as well as continuing to maintain his first wife and children.

'You can't afford to play games,' he said, in reference to his third marriage. 'Ros knew exactly what she was getting into right from the word go.'

Ros nodded in agreement. 'It was his honesty that impressed me,' she laughed.

The Bible is quite clear on this subject: a first wife set aside in preference for a second has full right of maintenance[4], as do the children born to her during the first marriage[5]. Anyone who fails to provide for his relatives, and especially for his immediate family, is roundly condemned[6]. But this doesn't stop the hassle that often continues between ex-partners. Maintenance can often be a source of ongoing sparring, leaving those involved with a longing to be able to manage without.

'It's always been a red rag to a bull,' Isobel said of her ex-husband.

'Yes,' Warren agreed. 'It would be nice if we didn't have to bother.'

Herein lies the problem. Notwithstanding the moral issues concerning fathers continuing to support their off-spring after the severance of the relationship with their mothers, and the children's own need to know that they have not been abandoned by their father passing his responsibilities over to another man, most often it is sheer economic necessity that makes maintenance, and all that it involves, the only practical solution.

Sorting out the labourers

One consideration to be made in the economic arrange-ments, will be whether the wife should work or not. This will depend upon several factors: Does the marriage neces-sitate moving away from the area? Will there be young step-children to be accommodated in the general scheme of things? Are more offspring planned? Is paid employ-ment seen as being desirable to the fulfilment of the wife, and thus the welfare of the partnership?

Leaving these aside for the present, the most pressing need is to establish whether there is an economic neces-sity. There may have been a drop in one or both incomes due to the loss of pension or maintenance brought about by the remarriage. Or where there is an established claim against the income of either partner by the members of the first family, then clearly the economics may be entirely untenable unless a substitute is found.

For Cathy this was a fact of life. Because she was partially supporting her mother there was no possibility of her giving up work, even had she so desired.

'I was working prior to our marriage,' she explained, 'and it was a joint decision that I was to continue working full-time. I enjoy my work so there was no resentment.' She paused. 'But there was also an economic need for me to continue since the mortgage repayments on our new home were much higher than on the tiny house I had before I was married.'

Her husband, Max, was retired and had, prior to their marriage, lived in a small flat. Without Cathy's income they would have been unable to purchase the larger house which they both felt they needed.

'Max helps with the household chores,' Cathy continued. 'We decided he must share these if I was to continue working full-time. Sometimes the strain and tiredness of it all gets me down, but on the whole we both cope with it.'

For Laura too, there was the necessity to continue working, though she too loved her job. Again, it was a matter for discussion before they married.

'Laura used her work as a district nurse to show the Lord's love to a great many people,' Leslie told me fondly. 'She was loved by many of her patients and we always had a bottom drawer full of chocs at Christmas time—given by them in appreciation of all she did. But we were both happy for her not to work when she became pregnant. It was a joint decision and there's no longer any need financially.'

'Mind you,' Laura's eyes lit up mischievously, 'occasionally, when Leslie was out of work, I thought I'd have to work all my life.' She smiled and nodded in his direction. 'Then I claimed God's promise that my husband was to be my provider. That's when Leslie got this job!'

Despite the necessity for them to continue working, and the tiredness this caused, both women clearly enjoy their jobs. Where there is no clear distinction of economic necessity, the posing of certain questions may well clarify the situation. Can the wife cope with running a home and job? Will such an arrangement be to the mutual benefit of the couple, or will unnecessary strain be put upon the whole family?

Gillian, a young divorcee, finding herself in this position, came to ask my advice shortly before her marriage to Alan.

'I just don't know whether I should continue with my job or not,' she said in perplexity. 'In many ways I don't agree with working wives and I feel it's important that I should be home when Alan gets back. He works long hours and is physically drained at the end of the day. I don't want to be unable to meet his needs because I'm too tired myself but I'm just not sure what to do.'

Knowing that Alan had never before been married and was now about to take on responsibility not only for a new wife, but also her two little girls, I rather doubted the wisdom of landing him with too much responsibility too soon. His employment was, in any case, somewhat precarious. And though believing wholeheartedly in the provision of God, I do not believe we should put him unnecessarily to the test. It's one thing to live 'by faith' when we have a clear Word from the Lord, quite another to do it off our own bat, so to speak.

When we'd talked through all the pros and cons, Gillian concluded that the best solution would be a temporary compromise, and asked for a reduction in hours. Some two months later, after a good deal of prayer, a change around in her department made that a possibility. Already she is reaping the benefit of a shorter working day with more time and energy to devote to her family. Yet Alan is not faced with the daunting task of moving in one swift stroke from responsibility for himself alone to sole provider for a family of four.

As far as Paul and I were concerned, we both felt that since there was no real financial pressure, we preferred to have fewer luxuries for the sake of more time together. So apart from a short period after our marriage, when I continued with my office job in order to help my employer through a sticky time, I have not sought paid employment.

'I wouldn't stop you working if you really wanted to,' Paul said, 'but I must admit that having waited so long to get married, I'd love to think we could spend all my holiday time together.'

As a teacher, that thirteen weeks a year was no small consideration. For myself, having had one marriage where I had been a 'work-widow' seeing little of my first husband, I wanted us to be together as much as Paul did. We are too good friends to sacrifice one another's company for the sake of more money.

'Mind you,' Paul said, teasingly, 'I wouldn't want you vegetating. One of the things I love about you is your lively mind. But I don't think there's much fear of that, do you?'

Heavily involved in Christian counselling, and writing, I rather doubted it! And as it has turned out, this has been an excellent compromise, providing me with all the 'fulfilment' I could possibly require, whilst ensuring sufficient flexibility to accommodate all our needs of mutual companionship.

Financing the future

It must have been about nine months before Paul and I got round to thinking about wills and then not for the obvious reason—there was no 'little Williams' in the offing. It was simply that moving house had brought us into contact with a solicitor. Had we realised the complications which could have arisen in the event of one or other of us dying intestate, we would not have left it so long.

I remember years ago, reading one of Catherine Marshall's books in which she described the problems she had to face because her husband Peter had left no will and his entire estate had had to be frozen.

It seemed that he felt that to do so would display a lack of faith in God's ability to provide. Since then, I too, have met Christians who feel likewise. The idea of wills, life assurance, indeed any insurance, is anathema to them.

Yet God clearly demonstrated, in the story of Joseph, his provision for the future, not simply for one individual but for whole nations. Pharaoh's dreams of the fat and thin cows and the sheaves of corn,[7] were, in effect, a life assurance policy and a will drawn up by God. In Joseph's interpretation of those dreams, God spelled out: the nature of the 'estate' (a fifth of the harvest); the way in which it was to be 'invested' (stored in the cities); the trustees (appointed commissioners under the authority of Pharaoh, and ultimately Joseph); and the beneficiaries (the people of the land).

When God promises to meet all our needs, he does just that. But some of what he provides *today*, may be intended to be saved for the future. Unless we do so, we may be robbing our dependants of God's provision for them.

The situation is, of course, complicated by the fact of step-children on one or both sides. And what is often overlooked, is that it may be further complicated by legally imposed responsibilities towards the first wife. There are instances (though rarely these days), where an unmarried first wife has all or part of a life assurance made over to her by the Registrar or Judge as part of the divorce settlement. Payment of premiums must continue to be met by the remarried husband, and where the second wife is compelled by economic necessity to work throughout the marriage, a good deal of resentment may brew up.

Even where these circumstances do not prevail, first wives who have not remarried and are therefore in receipt of maintenance will almost certainly have a claim against the estate in the case of death. So too would the children of the first marriage, even if little or no contact has been kept up. These factors need to be known and understood by both partners of the second marriage. Frank discussion with a mutually trusted solicitor should help to ensure this.

'We each made wills,' Leslie told me. 'Laura and I agreed that I should make a token legacy for my two girls, and I have no doubt at all that Laura would honour my wishes.'

Jeff and Doreen also made wills, but this time split three ways.

'We've left one-third to each of our own children, and one-third to each other.' Doreen explained.

'But we've appointed trustees so the children can't "blow" it,' Jeff added. 'The money is to be distributed gradually during the years between their twenty-first birthdays and when they're thirty-five.'

When it came to Paul and I sorting out our wills, we were fortunate enough to have the help of a Christian solicitor in our church fellowship. Although it was too late for us, he told us that the ideal arrangement would be for the documents to be drawn up prior to the wedding, ready for signature at the same time as signing the Register in the Vestry.

Accidents resulting in the death of one or both newly-weds have been known to happen either before or after the honeymoon! Since marriage immediately invalidates all previous wills and testaments, children of one or other partner could be put through unnecessary delay and anguish in the settlement of the estate, in addition to the pain of bereavement.

Problems can arise not only for the children but also for the bereaved step-parent. I was working for an estate agent a year or two before my marriage to Paul, and witnessed the distress of one poor man. His wife's will named her children as her beneficiaries and when she died, naturally enough, they wanted what was theirs. Unfortunately, all that she had was tied up in the house she had jointly owned with their stepfather. The only way they could realise the capital left them was to push for the house to be sold. Thoughtlessness and insensitivity rather than harshness and greed made them oblivious to the feelings of the stepfather who had provided for them throughout most of their lives.

For months he struggled to find something within his means, since the sale of the house had left him with only half the capital. During the time he spent looking, costs continued to soar. When, eventually, a tiny flatlet came up, to add insult to injury he had to dispose of most of his furnishings and possessions due to lack of space.

In the light of this experience, I wanted to make sure that Paul was never placed in a similar position. Much as I love my children and know their fondness for their stepfather, I know only too well how easy it is to rationalise, to convince oneself that a certain course of action is not selfish but expedient. In years to come they might have to make a choice between stepfather and their own husband or children. With the help of a solicitor, other ways were found to ensure that they will be well taken care of.

Yet the reverse is also a possibility. For many mothers the extent of their estate is entirely dependent upon the divorce settlement from the first marriage. They may own nothing more than what has been passed on to them by the father of their children. Where this involves capital, property, investments, furnishings, jewellery, objects d'art or other possessions, they may feel that, in the event of their death, their children should be sole beneficiaries; that they alone should inherit what had been jointly their mother's and father's.

Indeed, to do otherwise may well brew up resentment between step-child and step-parent. The wicked step-father of Victorian fiction grew largely out of the fact that he could re-marry yet again, taking with him the fortune of his deceased wife without obligation to her poor unfortunate offspring, his step-children.

It requires little imagination to see how hurtful this must be. For any child to see the personal possessions or jewellery of their deceased parent (perhaps passed on to them by a grandparent), being left to a step-parent, with the possibility of its being disposed of to others, would wound even the most Godly. As far as I am concerned, Paul would be most welcome to remarry in the event of my death, but I would take exception to his new wife or children wearing the engagement ring bought me by my children's father, or the wedding ring passed on to me by my grandmother.

This sort of thing is unlikely to happen in any truly loving Christian home, but nevertheless, it is as well to specify exactly who is to be beneficiary to what.

'Apart from the legacies I've made for my two girls,' Leslie told us, 'I've made it quite clear to them that Laura must have by far the biggest part of what's left. Much of it is hers anyway, from the sale of her home and her mother's legacy.'

Where there are children on both sides from previous marriages, with the possible addition of other children born to the new marriage, a will becomes even more important. Just telling them who gets what isn't enough.

Someone's forgetfulness could open the door to untold resentment and friction in the future.

In the meantime, frank discussion of all these aspects prior to committing oneself to a second partner, may go some way to negating the possibility of future misunderstandings, unhappiness and possibly even the breakdown of the marriage.

Notes

[1] 1 Timothy 6:10
[2] Ephesians 5:23
[3] Proverbs 31
[4] Exodus 21:7–11
[5] Deuteronomy 21:15–17
[6] 1 Timothy 5:8
[7] Genesis 41

5

Forming the Framework and...

It was early one evening as the autumn sun was slipping behind the trees, sending its dappled light into the lounge. Penny was tentative about broaching the matter on her mind. Maurice had not long been home from work, and as if subconsciously knowing that what she had to say would not be well received, she jumped to her feet, seeking preoccupation in closing the patio doors.

'There's a fellowship retreat next weekend,' she said without turning to look at him. 'I was speaking to Bob earlier and he asked if we were going.' She fiddled with the bolts, her slight figure bent over as she concentrated hard on slipping them into place. 'I said I thought we would. Be nice wouldn't it?'

Silence ensued from the regions of the sofa where Maurice's fair, thinning head of hair was bent over his coffee.

'Wouldn't it be nice?' Penny continued brightly, turning back to seat herself beside her husband of a few months.

'Well...', he mumbled hesitantly. 'Where is this retreat?'

'Oh, only down the coast. It's not far. There wouldn't be much travelling involved. Anyway, I could drive.' Penny knew that with all the extra commuting caused by their living in her home-town, Maurice wouldn't look kindly upon a long journey.

'We could have a nice quiet weekend at home. We haven't had one for ages, and I've been looking forward to some time on our own.' Maurice set his cup on the table, his grey eyes flickering briefly in Penny's direction.

'I knew you wouldn't want to go.'

Diffidently, Maurice put a hand on his wife's arm to restrain her from charging off.

'I'm right, aren't I? You just don't want to go. And I've already said we would.' Penny's dark eyes flashed.

'Well, it's true I'm not that keen on that type of thing— all herded together in a hostel without any home comforts. It's not a very relaxing way to spend your time after a hard week's work. You forget, I had far too much of it pushed upon me in my youth.'

Penny knew of Maurice's ultra-religious upbringing, but it didn't help. 'And what about me?' Her voice rose self-pityingly. 'I've never had the opportunity before.'

'Well you go without me.' Uncomfortably, Maurice rectified his mistake but Penny was not to be so easily pacified.

'How can I?' she demanded. 'People would wonder what was wrong between us.' Fighting against tears of disappointment, she marched off to the kitchen.

The whole thing was getting out of hand. This was the first major row of their marriage and Penny felt vexed beyond measure. 'The trouble with him,' she thought self-righteously, 'is that he has no real spiritual depth.'

Not given to prolonged bouts of moodiness, her sulkiness lasted but a short time. She had to admit that Maurice was right on one thing; they had had innumerable calls made on their time, with fellowship folk seeking Penny out for help and advice, prayer and encouragement at all hours. Maurice knew few of them as yet and with his natural reserve did not easily make friends.

What with that and the additional travelling time extending his working day, further augmented by his need to travel later in the evenings so as to avoid the rush-hour, their time together was made shorter still. And because of Maurice's tiredness after his long day, what little they did have was not quality time.

It had been an upsetting row, one of those milestone occasions that are never forgotten, when the honeymoon fantasy is stripped away, and you see each other in stark reality. Though outwardly resolved eventually, still the ripples kept coming. And for Penny, that meant that those unworthy thoughts of Maurice's spiritual status continued to muddy the waters.

Undergirding

But the Divine Architect uses only the best materials. The iron framework of a modern building under construction may look rusty and brown as it stands in all its naked starkness, silhouetted against the sky; only the engineer knows its strength, tested and tried to remove all impurity, so that it can bear the weight of the cladding which will render it useful according to the purpose for which it was designed.

Only time would show that Penny's and Maurice's row was to be one of those multiple lessons the Lord sometimes uses for our growth. Tested and tried, with the impurities removed, the framework of their marriage had to be made strong enough to withstand the burdens of a stepfamily, and the battering of the elements of the outside world. Penny takes up the story of how that was achieved.

'It took me a little while to realise that the shape of the framework had to be right before it could support the building,' she told me. 'That meant that Maurice and I had to get our relationship right first. If there was any weakness in that area it would quickly be spotted by the kids, and once they started getting at us and driving a wedge in, I knew it would be the beginning of the end.'

Penny had read Charles Swindoll's book on marriage, *Strike The Original Match*, in which he points out the complexities in family relationships. It is usual in a first marriage to have some time for husband and wife to settle down to each others idiosyncrasies before the babies come along. With the advent of offspring, husband and wife now have to relate not only to each other as partners, but to each other as parents (which can spawn a whole new set of disagreements) as well as to each child personally. The children in turn have to relate to one another (with the inevitable sibling rivalry for their parents' attention) and to each parent individually.

For the stepfamily this is further compounded. The children are already there! There is no time for husband and wife quietly to become acquainted with the intimacies of rubbing along together. It all has to be done under the scrutiny of the offspring, and often with audience participation, whilst at the same time juggling all the other relationships. For now there are blood ties competing with the bonds of step-relationships, not to mention the spectre of a first husband or wife (father or mother to the children) lurking in the background. And as Doreen had found out when her daughter had so resented Jeff, the ties go beyond the grave, involving even those whose partner is deceased.

Opening up her Bible, Penny continued her story. 'First God had to deal with my self-righteousness as far as Maurice was concerned,' she began. 'It wasn't many days after our row that I read this verse from Romans 14:4: "Who are you to judge someone else's servant? To his own master he stands or falls. and he will stand, for the Lord is able to make him stand."

'It was almost as if God was chastising me for my arrogance: "Who do you think you are?" so to speak. Then I realised, that in one sense, Maurice's spiritual standing was none of my business—he was not my servant, but the Lord's. And what's more, my attitude was a slur on God himself. He had obviously accepted Maurice as his servant, who was I to decide that Maurice wasn't up to it?'

Penny put her finger on the verse before continuing. 'I double underlined some words in the second part,' she indicated, 'because I found it so encouraging. "He will stand, for the Lord is able to make him stand." Sort of puts me in my place doesn't it?' she smiled. 'It's obviously not going to be me who has anything to do with it. The Lord is already committed to doing whatever's necessary. I had a lot of repenting to do!'

From that moment on Penny had found herself able to accept Maurice just as he was, putting into practice the words of Ephesians 5:22: 'Wives, submit to your husbands as to the Lord.'

'I realised that Maurice and I had to get it right if our relationship was going to be a firm base for the family. And the only way that could happen was if we went back to basics. We spent hours talking and praying together and studied every book we could find on marriage. And it was so much easier submitting to Maurice—even when I felt he might be wrong—when I remembered that it was up to the Lord to sort him out, not me.

'And it put a whole new concept on submitting when I realised I didn't have to be a doormat. God still expected me to be a "help meet" for Maurice,' Penny finished, quoting from Genesis where God creates Eve from the rib of Adam.[1] 'As I submitted, Maurice actually began to appreciate how invaluable it was to have a God-given helper.'

Paul and I could relate to the sentiments Penny had expressed. In the early days of our marriage there were many times when he and I had differing notions—usually over some minor matter, such as where to site the new rhododendron we had just bought, or whether to paper or paint the dining room.

It was hard to let go, having for years been the sole decision-maker since my divorce. Though keen to establish Paul as head of the family, it had become almost second nature during those years alone to expect my way of doing things to go unchallenged. I had to learn too, not to allow the trivial to build up out of all proportion. But like Penny it had not taken me long to realise that having stated my opinion on the matter, and presented my case as well as I was able, it was better then simply to leave it. If it were a matter of some importance, I would pray, pouring my feelings out to the Lord and asking that he should overrule, so that it would not be my decision nor Paul's which prevailed, but God's.

Perhaps five times out of ten, sometimes more, sometimes less, Paul would come to me an hour, a day or a week later.

'I've been thinking about that matter we were discussing last week,' he'd say with some embarrassment, 'and I think you were right. It would be better to follow your suggestion.'

Nowadays, emboldened by familiarity, he teasingly refers to his absolute inability to cope without his 'help meet'.

Occasionally, very occasionally, he would tell me he had been thinking through some matter or other, and would then present my suggestion as if it were his own, having completely forgotten that we had had any previous discussion. It hasn't happened often enough for me to get too excited about, though I sometimes give him a gentle and teasing reminder as to who was the genius who came up with that particular solution.

Of course, it does happen in reverse. Sometimes it is I who have to go to Paul, having had to revise my opinion in the light of his argument. Occasionally, in either case, the change of heart has come too late for the decision to be altered. We have then had to write it off to experience and forgive each other for the disappointment.

But we realised early on that one of the essentials of a successful relationship is to learn that 'my way' is not the 'only way', nor even, necessarily, the 'best way'. Rather than seeing our partner's viewpoint as being in opposition to our own, we have come to appreciate it as an extension to our thinking power and creativity, in much the same way as adding a greater kilobyte memory to our computer would be. Opening the mind to what God has to offer through one's partner can be one of the most rewarding and marriage-enriching experiences.

Having realistic expectations

There were still more lessons to be learned from Penny's experience as she continued to relate to us. During the weeks following the row she began questioning what she had expected from Maurice, and whether her expectations were rooted in his true personality and potential or in some fantasy image she carried in her mind as to how she would like him to be.

'Just before Maurice and I met,' she explained, 'I'd realised that most of the men I'd been out with during the years after my divorce were very similar in temperament to my ex-husband. Although I'd had a very unhappy first marriage, it seemed as if I was still attracted to the same type.

'I only woke up to what was happening when I found a man friend giving me the same bad time my 'ex' had given me. I suddenly thought: "Hang on. Whatever are you doing? If the Tom, Dick and Harry you've been going out with are the same type as the man you were divorced from, then it stands to reason they're going to give you the same run-around as he did." '

She laughed. 'I probably would never have accepted Maurice's advances, when we met through friends, had it not been for that realisation. He was so completely opposite to everything my first husband had been.'

Paul and I nodded in empathy. We'd recently read Tim De La Haye's book *Understanding the Male Temperament*, and had realised, as never before, that for every 'positive' in a personality there is an equal 'negative'. Like the two sides of a coin, the individual has his two faces.

Maurice, for instance, was a home-loving man, quiet, cautious and gentle. He was, in fact, everything that Penny needed after the hurts of her first marriage. But at the time of their row, her disappointment had impaired her vision so that she'd seen his good qualities in reverse.

'I realised later, that I had wanted him to be dynamic—really involved in that weekend retreat and a spiritual leader of men,' she explained. 'But he couldn't be that and have all the qualities I so loved in him. If he was going to be rushing off being dynamic all over the place, he couldn't also be the home-loving man I married. Not only would he not have the inclination, there simply wouldn't be time for gardening and decorating and all the things we loved doing together.

'Maurice loves the quiet togetherness of just being with me, whereas my "ex", who was a dynamic "leader of men", used to hold forth in the pub every evening whilst I sat in.' Penny's eyes dulled as she remembered her unhappy past.

'But that wasn't all,' she continued. 'I'd even begun to see Maurice's cautious approach to money as meanness, until I remembered how we'd always been in hock up to the eyebrows in my first marriage.'

She sat for a moment before regaining her composure. 'Mind you,' her eyes twinkled, 'I think Maurice and I are good for each other. He does sometimes need a gentle prod from me, to be a bit more generous, just as I sometimes need his restraining hand in other ways.'

******

However bad the first marriage has been, it is all too easy for the divorcee to be inadvertently drawn into having false expectations of the new relationship. It is vital that this should be recognised and come to terms with before anything damaging can be said. No one in a loving relationship wants to hurl hurtful and unfair comparisons at their partner—'Ferdinand may have been in debt up to his neck, but at least *he* brought me flowers, which is more than you do'—but there is always that unguarded moment to beware of.

Better, by far, to be clear from the start what your new partner's strengths are, and to build on them, gently encouraging the strengthening of those weaker parts. What a privilege we have to be party to what God is doing in our loved one's life, and to see the blossoming of that personality into something of strength and beauty.

But it is not only the divorcee who may have problems in this respect. Unfavourable comparison may, in fact, come easier to the widowed, whose memories of the first marriage may be of fondness and, therefore, more of a sense of loss. Seeing the deceased partner in hindsight, through rose-coloured glasses, may give a very jaundiced view of the second spouse.

Though there may be some feelings of guilt associated with things left undone, words left unspoken, or even the odd angry word which is later regretted, memories for the widowed will be, for the most part, cherished remembrances of happy times. Where the divorcee sustains hopes of something better in a second relationship, the bereaved, perhaps nursing continuing feelings of guilt

and disloyalty, may compare the new spouse unfavoura-
bly. Any attempts at countering this may manifest itself as
behaviour designed to drive away the 'usurper'. Seeking
counselling and a healing ministry may be the only way in
which this can be resolved.

For both the widowed and divorced there is a need to
establish with the new partner a policy concerning reference to the first marriage. Though comparison between
each relationship to the detriment of the second spouse
should never be indulged in, it is virtually impossible,
without cutting out a whole section of one's life, never to
make any reference to the past. Nor, especially where
there are children involved, would this be desirable.

The new marriage should be secure enough to withstand normal, unstilted conversation which may include
events that took place in the first relationship. Photo-
graphs, gifts, and memories cannot simply be obliterated.
And inevitably, particularly during the early years when
the second marriage has little or no 'history' to draw upon,
dinner-party conversation will contain snippets of a past
which excludes the new spouse.

Again, the importance of discussion cannot be over-
emphasised as a means of waylaying insecurity. The second spouse needs to understand that there is no intention
on the part of the other to offend or upset. Though it must
be said that women, in this context, due to a far greater
underlying insecurity than men, are less likely to feel
happy with dinner-party references to a past which
excluded them, they should, for the sake of the children,
be able to rise above their own feelings when it comes to
normal conversation regarding the ex-spouse.

As Doreen reminded us: 'Jeff has always said to me that
if there's anything I want to say about my past or com-
ment on in his, I'm just to say it. And the same goes for
him.

'I wouldn't be jealous or resentful because, after all, we're the ones living together now.'

Notes

[1] Genesis 2:18.

6

...Putting It In Place

One further lesson came out of Penny's and Maurice's upset. Once a true reconciliation had taken place, based on Penny's discoveries and repentance, Maurice was able to admit that his motives in not wanting to go to the fellowship retreat had not been entirely altruistic. Although he had quite rightly pinpointed their need for time quietly on their own together, this was not the whole story. But this was not to come to light until after one further upset in their lives.

Round pegs and square holes

About six months after the first event, the time came when both Maurice's and Penny's houses were sold and they were able to look for their first jointly-owned home. Obviously this had to be in Maurice's hometown since he was the only member of the family with a job to be considered and could hardly be expected to continue with all the commuting.

Deep down Penny did not want to move. She liked her town, her home and her fellowship—all so different from Maurice's. But she accepted that it had to be. And God was gracious, finding for them the house of their dreams. Despite her misgivings, Penny was thrilled as together the two set about creating their Ideal Home and Garden from the previously neglected premises.

They had been in residence for less than a month, and were still two months off their first anniversary together, when Maurice received a 'phone call one evening.

'That was my old badminton partner,' he explained delightedly to Penny. 'She wants to know if I'll rejoin the club now I'm living back in town again.'

Penny instantly dissolved into tears. It was all too reminiscent of her first marriage, and memories of her husband's frequent absences from home—passed off with plausible excuses but in reality a cover-up for his constant infidelities—crowded in upon her. The trouble was, she couldn't explain all this to Maurice. And he, bewildered at what he saw as her unreasonable and clinging demands, flared up with uncharacteristic ferocity.

Nor, for some weeks, was he able to understand his bride's daily depression and weepiness. It all, eventually, fell into place. Returning one day from a shopping trip in the village, Penny broke down in her husband's arms.

'Everywhere I go I see people relating to each other,' she wept, 'women, with their shopping baskets, standing on the pavement chattering away together, neighbours chatting over a coffee in the local cafe, mothers in jeans nattering together outside school as they wait for their children.' Here a great gulping sob interrupted Penny's outburst. 'And...I know...no one,' she finished at last.

As they talked later, Maurice realised that he had uprooted Penny (and her children) from their own home-town, set them down in his environment and simply expected them to get on with it.

'We were living in the town in which I'd grown up from childhood, and going to the church in which I'd been a member for over twenty-years. What friends I had—and I don't make many close friends—had known me all my life. Penny had no one.'

In her own hometown Penny had been actively involved in so many ways: her part-time job had kept her occupied three days a week, voluntary work in the fellowship coffee shop, membership of the counselling team, housegroups and fellowship with friends had given her a sense of worth and esteem. She was someone.

All that had gone. Alone all day, her only pursuits— doing up the garden and house—had further isolated her. The children were of an age where they took themselves to and from school, and besides, they too were having their problems in settling. Who, but Penny, could help them through that? Even in the church it seemed there was no place for Penny. Perhaps because everyone had known Maurice so long, and because he kept himself to himself, they expected Penny to do likewise?

Penny's problems took a little while to be resolved. Gradually she found her niche in the church where her gifts could be used for the Lord. Together she and Maurice found a joint ministry. And inevitably, those friends whom Maurice had as a single man tended to drift away whilst Penny and Maurice as a couple made new friends together.

'If I'm honest,' Maurice later recalled, 'part of my rejection of the fellowship weekend retreat before we'd moved was to do with it being on Penny's stamping-ground. It may sound ridiculous for a man to speak of insecurity, but frankly, I did feel like a fish out of water amongst Penny's charismatic friends. Sadly, it just didn't occur to me that Penny must feel likewise when the situation was reversed.'

Both Maurice and Penny readily identified with the wife of another couple. Doreen had continued to live in her marital home after her husband's death, but when she married Jeff she sold up and moved twenty miles away from home into his house.

'I really regret it now,' she confessed. 'I wish we'd both

sold up and bought something together. Even though Jeff's first wife had never lived there—Jeff bought the house after his divorce—I just felt like a lodger. To me it's Jeff's house, he makes all the decisions, and I don't feel free to change anything.'

'I don't know why,' Jeff interjected mildly, 'I always told you to change the furniture around as you want it and to be free to do whatever you like.'

Turning to us, he explained. 'To me, a home is not a home without a woman in it, and she puts her influence into everything. If Doreen chooses to do things in a certain way, then that is how it should be.'

Doreen had felt very homesick when she'd remarried, having previously spent all her life in one place. 'I was so lonely,' she recalled, 'I had to keep going into town just to get away from the four walls of the house. But I felt just as bad there. Everyone seemed to know someone except me.'

Doreen's solution was to find a job, but Jeff wanted her to be at home to answer the phone for his business. 'His mother had always done that before,' Doreen told us. 'I didn't want to risk her coming back and taking over so I didn't dare mention anything to Jeff to begin with.'

Eventually a compromise was reached. Doreen's father had a mid-week vacancy in his business, so it was agreed that she should take that up whilst Jeff would work from home that day in order to man the telephone.

For Ros, following on after Simon's first two wives, the situation was rather different. 'It was the stigma of living in sin, rather than the house,' she explained. 'Simon said it was my home and I could do whatever I liked. But one night when I couldn't sleep, I came down and put all the pictures and ornaments that had belonged to his second wife in a box. Simon came down and found me. He asked what I was doing. I said, "You told me I could," and he said, "Yes—but couldn't it wait till morning?" '

We all laughed. 'So living in what had been Daphne's home wasn't a problem?' I asked.

Ros thought for a moment. 'Not really to begin with...'

'It got worse the longer we were there,' Simon interjected.

'When we moved,' Ros agreed, nodding her head, 'I realised it had never really been a home.'

Great sensitivity needs to be shown in those early months of marriage if the relationship is to form a sound base on which to build the family. Even where discussion has preceded decisions—regarding all important matters such as where to live—those decisions have to be activated and coped with.

Inevitably it will take time to put down new roots, but it is essential that support be given to the uprooted partner. This is particularly so if there are also children to be rehoused and reschooled. If their parent is having problems adjusting and is therefore unable to help them, the stability of the whole family unit will be threatened. That support can only be given if each partner is aware of the other's underlying feelings and needs. And that requires time—time for each other.

Interior design—spatial relations

The pressures of creating time alone together are far greater for the stepfamily than for those in first marriages where partners at least have some months or years prior to starting a family. In the stepfamily the children are already there—a ready-made fomentation of future conflict brought about through unfinished conversations, unresolved arguments, and misunderstandings.

It seemed that whenever we began an important discussion, up would pop one or other of the girls. It was almost as if their fine tuning were switched on to our need to be alone, and that they were drawn like a moth to a candle to snuff out the flame. Disconnected conversations create tensions of their own but are nothing compared to the frustrations of fragmented arguments which leave you both up in the air, having to smile benignly at the intruder.

Of course, guilt is at the root of these added pressures. Where, in the 'natural' family mother and father would simply tell the children to buzz off, trusting that their basic security would protect them from being hurt, in the stepfamily there is always the underlying fear of a lack of security which will leave them vulnerable to feelings of rejection. There is a constant battle too against a fear of setting up jealousy or resentment on the part of the children toward their step-parent.

In one sense, the older they are the more difficult the problem. Little children can be tucked up in bed leaving parents free to share time quietly together. Babysitters can be called in to enable parents to have an evening out—a summer evening's walk, or a candle-lit dinner à deux. But unless your teenagers are social starlets they'll be there with you, wanting their own choice of TV programmes— Top of The Pops when you'd prefer Beethoven's Pastoral on the stereo—or inviting all their friends round and leaving an empty biscuit tin and endless dirty mugs.

All these things are taken in their stride by first-time-round parents (give or take a nervous breakdown or two). They've had time to get used to the idea, and to each other. Only a mother can fully appreciate the anguish and guilt of choosing between the time you want alone with your new husband and the time you know your children want with you.

'That's an area of disagreement between Isobel and I,' Warren shared with us one evening. 'I feel we put the children first too often. We should sometimes say: this is what we're doing and let them get on with it.' He pushed back his dark hair.

'After all,' he continued, 'in a few years time we'll be on our own and just have each other. We've got to build a relationship now.'

Isobel turned to me. 'We converted a bedroom so the kids had somewhere to watch TV with their friends if we have people in,' she said.

Talking to other couples confirmed these thoughts.

'Creating time together?' Simon answered, 'That's been more of a problem of late, with the children getting older and our commitment to the fellowship.'

Ros nodded in agreement. 'My days revolve around seeing people in the fellowship, seeing to the children, and the housework. Simon used to come home, eat, help me get the kids to bed and we would just want to flop in front of the telly. Our lives never got interwoven.'

'We always know when we've neglected each other,' Simon said seriously. 'A sort of dryness creeps in. I've had to learn to communicate with Ros. I'm old fashioned,' he smiled sardonically, 'protecting the little wife from the problems and pressures of business...I feel there's a loss of manliness if I talk to her about it. But I know really that it helps.'

This is not a problem simply of time together, but of quality time together. One way in which Paul and I sought to achieve this, carving prime time together out of the little time we had alone, was to attend marriage enrichment classes. There are organisations offering a weekend residential course but we chose a more pro-tracted arrangement which would not necessitate leaving the girls.*

By committing ourselves to two hours a week over a period of six weeks, we managed to guarantee at least one evening in seven focusing totally on our own relationship.

---

* Addresses are given in the Appendix.

There, we learned skills in communication—how to avoid that 'I know you believe you understand what you think I said, but I'm not sure you realise that what you heard is not what I meant' with which we can all identify; how to handle conflict creatively; and positive stroking—encouraging and building one another up as we are admonished in scripture.

Not all couples would feel happy with such group dynamics but all should seek to have some prime time alone together on a regular basis. Sympathetic towards the pressures experienced by couples like Ros and Simon, I asked if they ever managed to have an evening out together.

Simon nodded. 'We're really lucky having Ros's mum to relieve us.' He laughed uproariously. 'Of the three, she's the best mother-in-law I've ever had!'

******

Penny and Maurice's children were in their teens so the problem of babysitters didn't arise. Even so, they found problems of a different nature—that of showing affection to one another.

'You never seem to give me a hug these days since we got married,' Penny complained mildly one day. Naturally demonstrative herself, she turned from the drying-up and put her arms around Maurice as he stood at the sink.

'No, I suppose I don't,' Maurice admitted putting his arms around his wife as best he could with soap-sud hands. 'I think I'm always worried about upsetting the girls.'

As if on cue, Melony, Penny's fifteen-year-old walked into the kitchen.

'Hey,' she said peremptorily, addressing her mother,

'you're always cuddling Maurice; you never give me a hug.'

Deliberately misunderstanding her, Penny kept tight hold of Maurice as he made to break away, but raising his arm with hers endeavoured to take Melony into their embrace.

'Come on then,' she said cheerfully. 'We'll all have a hug together.'

With great embarrassment Melony struggled and broke free.

'I just feel that she has to see us being affectionate to one another,' Penny explained later to Maurice. 'What an odd view of marriage she would have if she never saw us behaving as if we love one another. Her expectations of marriage would be quite false, with romance a non-starter.'

Maurice nodded. 'I agree in theory. But when it actually comes to putting it into practice, I'm so afraid of hurting her, making her feel excluded, or worse still, jealous of me.'

Penny and Maurice decided that they could not let these fears dictate their behaviour, and that as long as there never was any exclusion in their public cuddling, Melony would have no justification for feeling rejected. Despite her embarrassment, they continued to pull her into their embrace whenever the occasion demanded and Penny made sure she gave Mel as much individual attention as possible. Gradually, what could have become a major issue simply dissolved away.

But problems of another nature began to come to light in the need for different family members to show affection. Annabel, Mel's older sister, shared none of her inhibitions. Like her mother she was naturally demonstrative.

'I need a big cuddle,' she would say in a baby-voice to Maurice, and taking his arms would enfold them about her.

Penny could see Maurice's discomfort. It was one thing to give the girls a kiss on the cheek, or even to put an arm about their shoulders. But to take your grown-up step-daughter in such a close physical embrace seemed wrong to him.

'I can't define it,' he admitted later. 'It just doesn't feel right.'

Tactfully, Penny had to explain Maurice's misgivings to Annabel, passing it off as a personal inhibition on Maurice's part so that she should not feel hurt.

With endless patience, Maurice accepted the restrictions upon his time alone with his wife, to the point that it was often only because Penny insisted that they had any time of their own.

Inevitably the pressures build up so that even in the most loving stepfamily situation there are bound to be tensions. Some may indeed be due to the 'unnaturalness' of the stepfamily, others no more than what is already inherent in each family member. It may come as something of a shock to a previously unmarried man to discover that he has moods. He may deny categorically that he was ever roused to anger when he lived alone. But the fact is that marriage—first or second time round—does not actually cause behavioural problems. It only brings out what was already there.

When everything is given to God in prayer, it may be that he will use the marriage to reveal previously hidden characteristics. Those living alone are free to have their own way. Only in the sharing of family life may their selfishness be brought to light. Anger may be vented in solitude, but unless there is another being to reflect it back, one may be quite unaware of its existence in one's life.

The temptation to blame one's spouse (or step-children) for all conflict is paramount. But as John Powell wrote of a journalist asked why he reacted so pleasantly to the newsagent who was consistently rude to him: 'Because I don't want *him* to decide how *I'm* going to act.'[1] It is the way of the world to blame others for our actions and reactions. And it is this that invites the response of walking away from the one perceived as being the cause of our own moods and our inability to cope with the moods of others.

Only as we take responsibility for our responses are we free to love, despite the storms of life. And it is only in fully understanding the real meaning of love that the storms can be weathered.

Nuts and bolts

We are indoctrinated, in this day and age, into believing that the thrill of sexual attraction and romance is the essence of love. Victorian novelists, Hollywood razzmatazz, and the permissive society of the sixties have sold us on the desirability of 'twanging heart strings' and physical intoxication. Yet the dizzy, breathtaking sensations experienced in the early days of 'being in love', though they may continue from time to time throughout the duration of marriage, are not, in themselves, a strong enough base on which to build a durable relationship.

Much of this physical sensation (and here I am not speaking about sexual arousal), is caused by the novelty factor in a new relationship and inevitably lessens with familiarity. Given time, a deepening love (which is no less overwhelming on occasions) can take root, but this is dependent upon a deepening intimate awareness of the other's person—body, mind and spirit.

In the immediacy of the environment in which we now live, the expectation is for instant results. Getting to know another person at that deeper level takes time (and commitment) and this is a commodity in short supply these days. Yet the desire for love remains undiminished. It is the combination of these factors which causes so many marriages today to fail, driving its victims to change partners with an ever increasing frequency.

Mistaking the thrills of 'falling in love' to be the 'real thing', such people become 'hooked'. When the first thrill wanes they seek pastures new, not realising that the Tender Trap is only the aperitif. The feast which lies beyond is more satisfying by far. The problem is how to get the diner from cocktail cabinet to banqueting table! There has to be something more. Something which, having attracted a man and woman to each other, will insure that they stay together.

Nuts and bolts are designed to hold together the various components of building materials. Some things remain unchanged: that is, they are the same for first marriages as for second. Priorities and commitment are the nuts and bolts of any marriage. When all else fails, these two provide the fail-safe. It is in the nature of commitment that it is total. To say that one is partially committed is a nonsense.

We need look no further than the opening chapters of the book of Genesis (upon which much of the Canonical marriage ceremony is based) to see that God does intend marriage to be for life. There are many birds and beasts which simply mate and then split, one or other (usually the female) being left to rear the young. Others abandon their offspring before the gestation period. Marriage, unlike the union of the animal kingdom, is intended to be more than simply for procreation. Neither of these methods is, therefore, open to human beings.

Nor, despite the misguided conceptions promulgated today, is marriage intended to be only until 'lack-of-love us do part'. Not only did God intend that men and women should cleave together to become 'one flesh', but their union is to be a living testimony of the relationship between Christ and the church.[2] The relationship itself is symbolic of the strength and durability of God's love for his children. This, more than anything, is what commitment is about—the pledge which binds the two together through thick and thin.

The Concise Oxford Dictionary[3] speaks of commitment as being an 'engagement or involvement that restricts freedom of action'. Just as we might reply to an invitation: 'Due to a prior commitment, I am unable...', so must the marriage vows, voluntarily taken, restrict our freedom of action so as to maintain a fidelity which is absolute. That means that no thought of giving up can even be entertained.*

There is no coercion in a wedding ceremony. The wording is such as to ensure that each party enters freely upon this course of action, and that neither does so lightly. Each should understand the nature of commitment. And it is that very restriction upon the freedom of any action outside the marriage which gives absolute freedom within the marriage.

It means that before that first flush of romance begins to fade, a new depth of love must be founded, a growing sense of selflessness which puts the well-being of the other as a priority. Any action which is potentially damaging to the other must thus be restricted. And it is this voluntary restriction on your partner's side which gives you such confidence and freedom within the marriage, and your self-imposed constraint which gives them theirs.

Submission is the name of the game. We are told to 'submit to one another out of reverence for Christ.'[4] Submission, like commitment, is not a state imposed upon one, but a state voluntarily entered into. And it is not

---

* I realise that many of those reading these pages will be in the position of having already given up on one marriage, as I had. There is no condemnation intended, and I suggest that they read the last chapter before throwing away this book in disgust.

solely because of our love for each other, but because of our love for the Father, and reverence for the Son.

Jesus, as he prepared to submit to the cross, told Pontius Pilate 'You would have no power over me if it were not given to you from above.'[5] In loving obedience to his Father, to whom he had prayed in the Garden of Gethsemane 'Not my will but yours', he gave up his right to a life of his own. His submission was not to Pilate, but to the Father's authority vested in him.

For so long submission has been seen solely as the woman's part and confused with subservience—a position of inferiority. But Jesus was a man and I see no inferiority in him. Yet we read that husbands are to love their wives as Christ loved the church and gave himself up for her! Husbands, to my mind, have the far harder part, for they are called to model themselves upon the perfect Christ, accepting responsibility for the holiness of their wives.

The man's love for his wife is also likened to that which he has for his own body. She *is* his body, just as he is hers, since the two are now 'one flesh'. When your body is cold, you warm it, when it is tired you give it rest. A hungry body is fed, and when grieved you take comfort.

It makes no sense to deny these attentions to your wife. The happiness of each is dependent on the other. No man can truly be content whilst depriving his wife. She needs warming in her husband's love and respect, just like the Good Wife in Proverbs,[6] and understanding when fatigued. Her nourishment is the mental stimulation of a husband who seeks her opinions and avails himself of a wisdom and insight exclusively feminine.

When God said it was not good for man to be alone, he was, in a sense, acknowledging man's incompleteness. God is without gender. Yet to be made in his image required the creation of both male and female characteristics. It is, I believe, mankind which is made in the image of God. Because God encompasses all that is to be found in both genders, neither Adam nor Eve, without the existence of the other, could be said to portray fully the image of a Triune God. Nor, alone, could man enjoy a similar intimate fellowship as that enjoyed by Father, Son and Holy Spirit.

Imagine a world of all men! Strong, visionary, and courageous they might be. But how in the world could God ever have shown, through human beings, his other side? That motherly love that yearns like a hen gathering her chicks under her wings[7], that gentle lover whose love is more delightful than wine?[8] These are qualities which cannot exist in a vacuum. Their very survival is entirely dependent upon there being someone on whom to expend them.

Humanly speaking, all the Godly attributes of tenderness, compassion, fidelity, and sociability require the existence of another being to draw them out and develop them. This other being must be different from the self in order to eliminate the competitiveness that exists between those of the same gender. To paint a portrait in black ink on black paper is as useless as to do so in white ink on white paper. Nor can either exist alone. A piece of black paper is not a portrait, nor is white ink drawn in the air.

Only with the contrast can the picture be seen, and the relationship between each medium then becomes apparent. Together, they are a monument to the skill of the artist.

And so woman was created as a 'suitable helper'. She was to be the one upon whom those qualities could be spent and without whom they might wither and die. In the ideal world of the Creation, before the Fall, mankind, together with womankind, accurately and beautifully conveyed the skill of the Creator.

Charles Swindoll, in his book *Strike the Original Match*[9] points out that the word 'helper' is vastly downgraded in the English language. 'The Hebrew,' he writes, 'is much more meaningful. It conveys the idea of someone who "assists another to reach complete fulfilment." ' How foolish it would be to ignore or despise such a God-given gift!

But this is no Jezebel charter. Wives are to submit to their husbands 'as to the Lord'. As Penny discovered, it was often only her love for the Lord which enabled her to submit to her husband. Not to do so, she realised, put her out of fellowship with God.

Marriage then, before the Fall, was God's picture for the whole of mankind, of what heaven will be like for the Bride of the Lamb. God has given we women our husbands so that we may learn and demonstrate his way of how to respond to the Lord.

But where does this leave the unmarried? Are they to be left with a feeling of being incomplete? If there is no one to assist them to reach 'complete fulfilment', will they be forever lacking in some way?

Personally, I do not believe in the gift of singleness—I find that a cop-out. It is my belief that before the Fall it was God's intention for all to be married, and that it is only because of factors too numerous and complicated to be chronicled here (wars for one, and a recent report that excessive consumption of alcohol produces an imbalance in the sexes) that men and women are left to live out their lives in a single status.

However, that is not to say that I do not believe in the gift of grace in singleness. There are many more crippling experiences than being unmarried. Joni Eareckson Tada, a quadriplegic since her teens, lives her life in such a way as to give more joy to the world (and therefore blessing for herself) than many of us who are able-bodied and independent.

To the single, I believe, God gives a special anointing of grace, enabling him to achieve his purposes of transforming them into the likeness of Jesus, alone. Unlike their married sisters they are free to look to the Lord alone, rather than to a husband. And properly used that gift of grace can be a source of real blessing and joy to all.

But for most of us, I am convinced that it is only as we rub along together as husband and wife that God is able to mould men and women to attain to those qualities which befit the Bride of Christ. We are to be presented 'radiant...without stain or wrinkle or any other blemish, but holy and blameless.'[10] Far from decrying the differences we find in each other, we should rejoice in the fact that these are the tools God uses to achieve our holiness.

The differences between husband and wife are the buffing agent by which he turns us into beautiful gemstones, refining and polishing us so that we no longer have rough edges. As love develops—that divine love called Agape—the friction which may be experienced in the early years softens to a gentle buffing. Blended together as 'one flesh' we take on the attributes of the other just as yeast and flour blend to become bread. Neither, of itself, would be palatable nor wholesome.

We read in Philippians that we may be 'confident of this, that he who began a good work in you will carry it on to completion until the day of Christ Jesus.'[11] That is commitment. God will never give up on us. He is committed to finishing his task of perfecting our holiness. And it is through our commitment to each other in marriage that he can best achieve that end.

Perhaps the whole essence of priorities and commitment are best summed up in a letter I received sometime ago from Leslie:

'Right from the beginning,' he wrote, 'Laura made it clear that she would put God first in our marriage. Now that hurt me at first—but only for a very short period because I saw that she was, and is, right. God must come first in any marriage because, being human, we can soon lose our lustre in our partner's eyes. (I'm not a pretty sight first thing in the morning!)

'So, if we start off in the earthly fashion of "worshipping" the new spouse, we discover soon enough that he/she has feet of clay and then dissatisfaction/unrest can set in. With God at the centre you always remind yourself that you must see with God's eyes—and give him very real thanks for the super blessing he's given you. And God has blessed me so richly with Laura. She's got to read all this of course—but I'm not ashamed to tell the world I love her immensely!'

Notes

[1] John Powell, *Why Am I Afraid To Tell You Who I Am?* (Fontana, Copyright Argus Communications, Illinois).
[2] Ephesians 5:22–28
[3] *The Concise Oxford Dictionary* (Oxford University Press).
[4] Ephesians 5:21
[5] John 19:11
[6] Proverbs 31:10–31
[7] Matthew 23:37
[8] Song of Solomon 1:2
[9] Charles Swindoll, *Strike The Original Match* (Multnomah Press, Oregon)
[10] Ephesians 5:27, 28
[11] Philippians 1:6

7

The Living Quarters

'Morning Melony.' Maurice poured cereal into his breakfast bowl. Penny, on the other side of the kitchen, was
putting the finishing touches to her daughter's packed
lunch.

'I said Good Morning.' Maurice's voice took on a new
tone. Melony spooned sugar liberally over her cereal,
emitting only a mumbled grunt in response to her stepfather's greeting.

There was nothing remarkable about the occurrence as
far as Penny was concerned, though she did notice that
Maurice seemed a little agitated as together he and Mel
set off for their respective schools—the one as teacher, the
other as pupil. Waving them goodbye, she returned to the
kitchen to finish her own breakfast.

It was not until later that evening that Penny discovered that the morning ritual had, for sometime, been a
source of irritation to Maurice.

'I'm sorry Penny, but I just find Melony's rudeness in
the mornings quite inexcusable. She barely acknowledges
me and when she does it's usually only when you've
prompted her.'

'Me? Prompt her?'

'I don't think you realise you're doing it,' Maurice
smiled stiffly, trying to take the sting out of the words, 'but

you do tend to jump in rather than leaving it to me to sort out.'

He was right; Penny had to admit it. It had become a sort of second nature. In fact, if she was honest, though Mel was now fifteen, it was still a hangover from her primary school days when it had been natural as her mother to prompt her, 'Now say thank-you to Mrs So-and-so for having you darling...'

'I will try not to jump in,' she replied. 'But I'm still not sure I understand what the problem is?'

'Well, when I say good-morning to my class at school, they respond politely. The best I get out of Melony is a grunt.'

Penny smiled and laid her hand on Maurice's arm. 'I don't mean to excuse her but don't you see darling, you get a good response from your class at nine in the morning. What do you think they'd be like if you encountered them at seven when they're all grumpy and sleepy?'

Maurice nodded slowly. He had to acknowledge that there was some truth in what Penny was saying.

'And then there's the fact that you're their teacher. You can't expect to have the same sort of relationship with Mel—you're both living as a family now.' Coaxingly, Penny talked him through it. 'You must admit, it's only in the mornings she's like that. That's her low time. I don't suppose as a sisterless bachelor before our marriage, you've seen too many young women at that time of morning, have you?'

Maurice laughed. The situation had been successfully defused.

Familiarising yourself with the layout

There is an awkwardness about stepfamilies which takes time to resolve. For step-parent and step-child alike, new relationships have to be built up from scratch with adjust-

both sides. For a previously unmar-
adjustments are made even greater
to 'slot-in' to a ready-made family
ed alone as an adult, may be an
or them.

ll be times when the new member of
n/herself to be an interloper, intrud-
established behaviour patterns of the
mes natural defence mechanisms set
the uncomfortable feelings in any
ays. Irritation, aggressiveness, 'pick-
aily members, or simply isolating
an attitude of 'let them get on with
h my life', can soon become barriers
table proportions unless dealt with
it comes back to simple communica-

years seniority over her new hus-
ick up on his feelings, especially as he
life alone prior to their marriage.
the odd one out?' she asked Warren,
curls.
d with an air of confidence. 'No not
me to me when their bikes needed
uild cages for the rabbits...and so

too, were sensitive to the situation
n to take care of the two little ones
had abandoned.
oung ever to remember a time when I
Ros said. 'But Kevin reacted! He was
r, so he was very much on his Dad's
s been a special relationship between
moved in with Simon to see if I could
evin as my own children.'
ey react?' I asked.

Simon replied, 'It didn't take Kevin long to r
was better off. Ros was a much better mot⟩
Daphne.'

Jeff and Doreen, with teenagers to contend w
rather longer to adjust. To begin with Jeff accuse⟨
of moaning when she had left food for the chil⟨
they then left their dirty dishes all over the floor.
understandably enough, felt angry.

'I did more for Jeff's daughter than I did for r
she recalled.

Not until she and Jeff talked it through did they
a joint problem to be tackled together.

For Paul and myself, too, there were areas o⟩
ment. I remember on one occasion going to the ⟩
make Amanda's packed lunch, only to find that P⟩
late night binge the evening before, had demoli⟨
cooked sausages I had left at the ready. With litt⟩
fall back on that morning, a seemingly innocent an⟩
event turned into a minor crisis.

As a bachelor Paul had naturally enough
regarded the food in the fridge, which after all h⟩
bought with his money, to be at his disposal ⟩
reference to anyone else. Living as a family, the gi⟩
had become more used to the need of having to ⟩
how our actions would affect the other members.

Soft-furnishing—cushioning the knocks

But for all the settling in and adjustments the ste⟩
has to make, the transition is almost certainly far⟩
on the part of the step-child. Lacking an adult's
and maturity to deal with the hurts of the past, a⟩
split loyalties between both natural parents, as w⟨
the case of teenagers, their own physical, men⟩
sexual upheavals to contend with, they are far mo⟩
mercy of their emotions. Just at the time when h⟩

and wife are having to make major changes in their own lives, huge demands are made upon their resourcefulness in understanding and dealing with the needs of the children.

Penny and Maurice, already bewildered by Melony's odd behaviour in the early days of their marriage when Mel had seemingly regarded Maurice as her personal playmate, now found, a year or two on, that they had need of huge resources of insight.

'In her fifteenth year,' Penny recalled, 'Mel switched from being the little girl jumping all over her new step-father and became his personal dresser. The Action Man Syndrome had switched to the Little Wife Syndrome.

'It was uncanny, really.' Penny shook her dark head. 'Whenever Mel and I went out shopping together, she would nag me to buy Maurice something new. "Look at these, Mum," she'd say, indicating some really trendy trousers. "Get these for Maurice. They're much better than those boring old-man's trousers you usually get him." '

Maurice took up the story: 'She'd already cleared out my wardrobe,' he smiled affectionately. 'Insisted that she wouldn't be seen dead with me in some of my old favourites. All my platform shoes and flared trousers had to go. And she saw to it personally—all in the dustbin. Not that I really minded. I never wore them after all, I'd just hung on to them.'

'I'm glad she did clear them out,' Penny laughed. 'I wouldn't be seen dead with you in flares and platforms either. But you'd never have allowed me to throw them out, would you?

'Anyway,' she continued, 'every time Maurice and I went anywhere—even if she wasn't coming with us—she insisted on dressing him: chose which shirt he'd wear and which tie. She'd even put them on him, button them up and tie the knot in his tie.'

'Then she began cutting my hair,' Maurice smiled. 'Penny was always nagging me to get it cut before I thought there was any need. But I had to admit my sideburns used to get a bit shaggy, and there was always a bit at the back that began to get a bit unruly as it got longer. So Mel took to giving me a trim…'

'She'd sit him on a chair in the kitchen,' Penny interrupted, 'put a towel round his shoulders, and very carefully trim off all the surplus. Not a proper cut—just the untidy bits.'

'And a good job she made of it too!' Maurice said.

'You'd never have trusted me to do that, would you?' Good humouredly, Penny teased her husband. 'Anyway, the point is, that the more we talked it through, the more we realised that Mel needed to have physical contact with Maurice, and that because of her shyness, this was the only way she could overcome her inhibitions.'

'It was the same when she used to jump all over me,' Maurice agreed.

'There had obviously been a need for her to "fill in the gap" from when her father left.' Penny's dark eyes grew sombre. 'Quite simply, she didn't know *how* to relate to a man living in close circumstances as a member of the family, because her "education" in personal relationships, so to speak, had been interrupted when she was still quite young. She'd had to revert to the behaviour that was natural to her at the age she was before her father left, and gradually build upon it.'

We could understand Penny and Maurice's situation, since we too had seen that 'education gap' in personal relationships in our girls. Nor was it peculiar to them. Paul, too, had had to 'learn' how to be a parent—albeit a step-parent—of a teenager, since there had been no gradual evolution as with a natural parent. Whenever I'd encountered difficulties in parenting my eldest daughter, I'd often remarked to her, 'I'm bound to make a few mistakes and will have to learn from them because I've never been the mother of a...year-old before.' But where I'd had the experience of all the previous years to build upon, he had none.

Paul's answer had been to be 'laid-back', to use one of his favourite expressions, allowing the girls to come to him, rather than forcing himself on them. He had found, particularly with the youngest of my teenagers, that contrived situations or conversations had quite the opposite effect to the desired result. Pushing himself into their lives simply drove a wedge between them.

Eventually, quite naturally, football became the common ground between Amanda and Paul. It began passively, both watching the highlights on television (much to my chagrin), and gradually evolved into regular outings together to see the local team.

'For a long time Amanda spoke always of "your" team,' Paul told me. "Your team" and "your town". It was as if she were distancing herself from me. Though she still has her own preference when it comes to supporting teams, she gradually let the pointed references to "my team" drop.'

This mutual hobby took on new connotations which further increased healthy family relationships. Discovering my ignorance of players and techniques, and my mild abhorrence of the sport, Amanda began affectionately taking sides with Paul against me. A nudge-nudge, wink-wink relationship began to build up between them, with me the butt of their amusement and scorn.

'Mummy's hopeless, Paul,' Amanda would tease derisively. 'She doesn't even know who Kevin Keagan is.'

Knowing that this father/daughter affinity versus mother was a normal and healthy development in teenagers, I began to play upon my ignorance—though not too overtly. It would not have done to underestimate

Amanda's astuteness. Not that it was often necessary any-way, nor, with my genuine lack of enlightenment, within my means to do otherwise.

Paul's feelings of needing to be 'laid back' where the girls were concerned, were in stark contrast to Warren's experience with Isobel's girls.

'I filled the gap their father left,' he said frankly. 'I went for it. I didn't sit back and wait for it to happen.'

'I think you did more than fill the gap,' Isobel insisted, 'because their father never filled it in the first place.'

Since the children were so much younger in this situation than my own, this approach may have been more acceptable to them than the laissez-faire attitudes Paul adopted. Up to a certain point, the younger the child, the fewer the inhibitions, though the acute embarrassments of early teenage years do eventually give way to more mature and relaxed attitudes. As far as step-parents are con-cerned, most of the difficulties in relating to their step-children occur when the children are in their middle years, say immediately pre-puberty to late teens.

The master suite

Not all difficulties, however, can be so neatly laid at the door of step-parent and step-child. Frequently, the desire of the natural parent for 'normal' family life may be so strong as to set up barriers of a different nature. The tendency then can be to try to create entirely untenable relationships.

One father, anxious to reconstruct a family home sim-ilar to a bygone era of happy times, insisted upon referring to his second wife as 'mummy' to his now grown-up sons. No doubt his motives were based on his desire to take them all back to the boys' childhood when contentment had reigned in the household. But since the relationship between stepmother and step-sons had not begun until both sons were on the brink of manhood, there was something of pathos in his attempts. Perhaps there was too, a desire to grant his second wife a 'motherhood' denied her by age.

In an excess of enthusiasm, I have been guilty myself, on one or two occasions, of trying to thrust my daughters and my husband into an affectionate embrace when a simple kiss on the cheek, or a quick hug, came more naturally to both.

In another family, expensive gifts were given to the children as if they were from the father's second wife. The children saw right through the charade, knowing that the gifts had, in reality, been purchased by their father and that this was an attempt at 'buying' affection for the stepmother.

Though unwise, these yearnings for all members of the new family to 'gel' are understandable. Marriage and family life are the two earliest ordinances of God's creation, and despite the modernist approach in seeking to destroy its validity, it remains fundamentally at the core of human need.

What is needed, however, is a strategy on the part of the natural parent to 'set-up' the step-parent in the appropriate role. Stepmothers need to know that they can count on the support of their husband, at least in front of the children, whatever may happen behind closed doors. Likewise, mum needs to 'set-up' stepdad as head of the home.

My girls, used to seeking and deferring to my judgement and opinions during the years after my divorce, naturally enough, continued to do so after my remarriage. As far as they were concerned, I had for so long been sole decision maker, it simply would never have occurred to them to turn elsewhere. I realised immediately that if they were ever to gain any real respect for Paul, this had to be altered, so that they would look to him, rather than to me, for those decisions affecting the family.

'Go and ask Paul,' was the phrase most often on my lips in the early days, to the point where they might quite justifiably have supposed that I had taken leave of all capability. Time was short, in our situation, with the girls soon to leave home. My 'helplessness' had to be exaggerated in order to point them to Paul's authority.

One way in which this was achieved was in the matter of finance, already referred to in Chapter Four. Aware of the fact that in the days immediately following our marriage we would be living en famille in what had been my home, filled with my furniture, and that this could become a bone of contention with the girls, we took contingent action. If, as one day happened, one of the girls were to object to Paul's 'intrusion' upon *our* domain, we knew we would need an invincible 'defence'.

'This may be our house and our furniture,' I was able to respond, 'but it is Paul's home as much as it is ours. And since he pays all the bills that keep the roof over our heads and food in our stomachs, he has as much right as anyone to have his say.'

In reality, the fact that he was my husband alone gave him the right, but to a youngster's mind this may be too abstract a concept. Bringing it down to the nitty-gritty of finance makes it within the grasp of all children, since even the youngest has some understanding of money and will feel gratitude towards the one who supplies their sweeties and pocket money.

Though teenagers *may* resent feeling beholden to a step-father, with the right approach on the part of the mother they can be made to understand and appreciate how positively she views the lifting of the financial burden from her shoulders. And gradually, even the most reluctant of teenagers can hardly fail to feel otherwise.

So successful were we in this respect, that Amanda got

to the stage of teasingly chastising me if she felt that I was overspending on clothes for myself. 'I'll tell Paul,' she would threaten. And tell him she did, though knowing deep down that she was on safe ground since we had no secrets from one another anyway.

Skeletons in the cupboard

There are stepfamilies where insecurity is such that secrets become rife. The jealous 'wicked stepmother' of Snow White fame, is, sadly, no myth, but a caricature of real-life.

Charles was in his thirties when he married for the first time. The product of a broken home himself, he was well aware of the phenomenon of the jealous step-parent. And as such, was always very sensitive to the feelings of his step-daughters, zealously promoting their right of access to their mother.

'I don't want them ever to feel they can't have any time alone with you,' he told his wife Dot. 'I want them to know they can have a private conversation without me.

'I was very close to my father before he remarried,' Charles explained. 'I was only in my teens at the time, but from then on I was never allowed to be on my own with Dad. If he ever managed to get me on one side, my stepmother would somehow get wind of it and push in between saying, "What's all this about? Secrets?" It was dreadful.'

'Even now,' Dot observed, 'if ever Dad shows Charlie any affection, she's there at once, just like a child, wanting to know where her kiss is.'

Charles nodded sadly. 'When it comes to borrowing tools or anything,' he admitted, 'it has to be done without her knowledge. It's as if she's terrified that anything that goes on between Dad and me robs her in some way.'

'Sometimes he slips a fiver in my hand as a treat for us,' Dot said, 'but he always warns me not to let Mum know.'

The situation was even more stressful in another situation. Evelyn, a small, homely woman in her forties, received a shock telephone call one day to say that her daughter, Val, was desperately ill in a London hospital and not expected to live the night. She attempted to trace her ex-husband, Dennis, to let him know.

'When I eventually tracked him down,' she told me, 'he seemed to be terribly reluctant to go with me to see our daughter, despite the fact she had lived with him and his second wife for sometime in the past. He kept questioning me and seemed to doubt the severity of the situation even though I told him I'd had three 'phone calls and been told it was a matter of life and death.

'Eventually, after what seemed endless consultations with his second wife, he agreed that we should go to London together. We got there quite late at night after all the delay. Our daughter was in intensive care, all wired up to heart monitors, arterial lines, intravenous drips and oxygen mask, but, praise God, she was alive and able to speak to us.

'As her situation was no longer quite so critical, the staff urged us to go to bed and offered us a room in the hospital. It had been a terrible strain, despite all the prayer I knew had gone up on our behalf, and I was dreadfully tired after the long journey. Knowing I would need all my strength for the coming days, I was happy to give in to Sister's suggestion.'

Evelyn twisted her hands in her lap. 'The room we were shown to had twin-beds at opposite ends. There was a bathroom, so we had some privacy, and when I'd changed into my night clothes, I got into bed. Dennis, in the meantime, had gone to feed the parking meter—and himself. I can't say I felt at ease at the prospect of sharing a room with him, but somehow, Val's illness seemed too important for the sleeping arrangements to have much significance. I was just grateful to get some rest.

'Dennis didn't come in until about four in the morning and then he only lay down on the other bed fully clothed. At about six, he made some coffee for us both. "I don't want this to get back to Theresa," he warned me. "She wouldn't understand at all." Actually, I felt rather sorry for her. I told Dennis that she had no need to feel insecure on my behalf, that I was now happily married myself and had no designs on him, my ex-husband. What's more, I told him, I would feel quite free to share the incident with my new husband.

'And then I asked Dennis if Theresa had been reluctant to let him visit his daughter when she was so critically ill,' Evelyn continued. 'I was quite amazed when he admitted that that was so, and that as far as Theresa was concerned she would rather that there didn't have to be any contact.' Evelyn shook her head in disbelief.

Unlocking closed doors

All the situations we came across seemed to feature the insecurities and jealousies of stepmothers, rather than stepfathers. Could it be, we wondered, a predominantly woman-oriented problem? Is there something in their make-up which makes women more susceptible to a lack of emotional assurance?

It may be because of the curse put upon mankind after the Fall in the Garden of Eden that women tend to be more vulnerable in this issue. 'Your desire will be for your husband, and he will rule over you,'[1] God pronounced over Eve. It would seem that we have been left with an overwhelming sense of low self-esteem, inferiority, insecurity and a jealous need for the undivided attention of our husbands.

If, as seems likely, this is the root cause of a woman's

insecurity, jealousy and low self-esteem, then it is good news. Good, because in acknowledging its source, we are handed the weapon for its defeat. For in Christ, we are told, we have freedom—freedom from the curse of the law. Jesus is the new Covenant, and the curse no longer holds us in its power. In him we live and move and have our being.[2] It is for freedom Christ has set us free[3], and if the Son sets you free, you will be free indeed.[4]

It is the enemy who seeks to apply the curse in our lives, who by the power of suggestion and manipulation of our emotions ties us up in condemnation, insecurity, jealousy and lack of self-worth. But for each shackle with which he renders our liberty useless, there is a key. Where guilt is the culprit, we may come to Jesus and know forgiveness; our insecurity, jealousy and inferiority are undone when we know ourselves loved by the Father, just as we are[5], sons and daughters of the King, co-heirs with Christ[6]. In Jesus name, we have all power and authority to come against the works of the devil.[7]

One stepmother who seems to enjoy the freedom won for her by Jesus is Ros. Knowing Simon's need to have time with his children, there seems to be no hint of envy in her behaviour.

'I play snooker with Kevin once a week,' Simon told us, 'and Ros spends time with Patsy. In our busy Christian lives, it's your family who gets left out.'

Simon paused in thought. 'I remember one of our elders saying there's got to be a time to stop commanding and start communicating with your children. I feel we've done that—going out regularly together and playing snooker. We've got a good relationship. We can talk about anything. I've even told Kevin if he wanted to live with his mother any time, he could. I wouldn't stand in his way.'

Ros smiled her approval. 'Kevin's a sensible boy, and a reasonable boy. He might go through a teens rebellion but

I don't think it would be because his parents have split up, but just because he's a teenager.'

Simon's ability to talk to his son about his natural mother opens up the way for honest dialogue between the two. There are no locked closets in their relationship, and young Kevin is never left with the feeling that his mother is persona non grata, nor that the mention of her name will cause any embarrassment. With the best will in the world, this takes skill on the part of the step-parent and custodial parent. Children are quick to sense any awkwardness.

Warren shared his own experience as a stepfather: 'Tracy always felt she could talk to me about the divorce, whereas she couldn't to her mother for fear of upsetting her. In that sense, I was like an outsider.'

'You never told me!' Isobel countered.

Warren lifted a hand deprecatingly. 'That's how I felt it had to be. She wanted a private conversation. If it had been something important I'd have told you,' he added.

This experience was shared by Jeff and Doreen. 'Natasha tells Doreen more than she tells me,' Jeff admitted.

'But it makes it awkward for me,' Doreen countered, 'because I don't like to keep things from Jeff. Sometimes if she has shared something with me and I tell him, he goes straight back to her to try and sort it out. I've told him I've got to be able to share things with him without him taking it back to her, otherwise she won't trust me.'

This sort of confidence can only be built up gradually, and its success is evidence of the way in which a stepfamily can become, not simply a botched-up or patched-up version of family life, but a completely new entity with a valid and worthwhile contribution to each member's growth and well-being. Establishing bonds in the wider family is further evidence of the fruitfulness of these new relationships.

'Laura's parents very quickly showed their love to me and my daughters when we married,' Leslie shared with us, 'and they have done so ever since. They have always included Hilary and Shirley in all family invitations which are extended to Laura and me. That wasn't lost on the girls last year when their natural cousins did not invite them to a wedding to which Laura and I had been invited. In the end, we decided not to go either rather than hurt them.'

In Jeff and Doreen's family, it was the siblings who reached out to form new relationships. With Jeff's daughter's eighteenth birthday imminent, Kirstin, Doreen's daughter, unable to find a card saying 'Sister', wrote it on herself and sent it to Natasha.

'All my family bought Christmas presents for Natasha too,' Doreen told us. 'She was quite overwhelmed.'

With such love and acceptance from step-parents and from wider family alike, one would hope that there would not be too much in the way of conflict in the future.

Notes

[1] Genesis 3:6
[2] Acts 17:28
[3] Galatians 5:1
[4] John 8:36
[5] Romans 5:8
[6] Romans 8:17
[7] Mark 16:17 and Luke 9:1

8

Faults with the Fittings

'You'll have to think very carefully about what you're going to do,' the doctor told Penny over the telephone. 'I know it sounds harsh, but children in Stacey's situation can be real home-wreckers. It's not even as if she's a child. She left home some years ago, after all. And you've got Maurice to consider. Do you want your second marriage to go down the drain?'

Penny shifted the receiver to the other ear. 'I know what you're saying,' she sighed, 'but what option have I but to take Stacey in? I'm the only mother she's got. If I don't help, who will?'

'Well, it's your decision, but I certainly think you must find out how Maurice feels about it. Remember, she's not his daughter.'

Much as she valued the opinion of her doctor-friend, Penny couldn't help but feel that it had its limitations. As a non-Christian he couldn't possibly understand that extra dimension of having a Father on whom to cast one's cares, nor, as a man, could he comprehend the eternal quality of that invisible umbilical cord which links all mothers with their children irrevocably.

'I'll have to think about it.' Forcing a smile into her voice Penny bade the doctor goodbye, replacing the receiver.

She'd have to talk it through with Maurice of course. Taking a drug-addict into your home was no small consideration. But wasn't this part of the 'for better, for worse' that Maurice had promised in their marriage vows?

That was all very well. But would she, Penny, have the grace to include Maurice's wayward relatives in their family home should the occasion arise? As Maurice had no children, the whole question was somewhat hypothetical. But even so... Aware of her need to show great sensitivity, and truly allow Maurice freedom to refuse her request for Stacey to move in, Penny bowed her head and began to pray.

'I told the doctor Stacey wants to come off the drugs,' she told Maurice frankly that evening, 'but he says all addicts are notorious liars. Darling, I can't bear the thought of refusing to help her, but it has to be a joint decision. I'll understand if you say no. This is your home as much as mine and it wouldn't work unless we're in it together.'

Maurice didn't reply immediately. Anxious though she was, Penny realised that this was a good sign; that he was not simply going to jump in with his agreement in order to pander to her wishes, and perhaps regret it later.

Several months on, when Maurice had given his agreement and Stacey had been living at home for some time, Penny was to be even more grateful for the time Maurice had given to consider the matter. It would have been hard-going living on a knife edge with a drug addict even under normal circumstances; in a stepfamily that was intensified, every little nuance of behaviour taking on a new connotation.

There was the matter of Stacey's smoking. Neither Maurice nor Penny smoked, though both had in the past. Waking in the early hours of the morning on one occasion, Penny discovered Stacey in bed, out for the count, with a lighted cigarette in her hand burning a hole in the bedding.

'It was a miracle I woke and went into her bedroom at all,' Penny later related to Maurice. 'I mean, I'd no reason to go in.'

'It's a miracle we weren't all burned alive in our beds,' Maurice agreed gravely. 'I think you'll have to tell Stacey there's to be no more smoking in the house.'

'Not at all?' Stacey grumbled when Penny relayed Maurice's decision. 'Not even if I come down to the lounge?'

'Darling, you're just as likely to fall asleep in the armchair and set it alight,' Penny gently rebuked her daughter. 'You'll have to go into the garage when you want to light up.'

In a two-parent family, Penny knew there would not have to be all this relaying of information. A natural father would feel free to express his own ultimatums to his daughter without constantly having to go through his wife. It took its toll on Penny, all this being piggy-in-the-middle, but she knew it was just as difficult for Maurice. The dark circles under his eyes were enough to tell her that his usually sound sleep was disturbed by his fears for the safety of home and family. Together, the two of them took to praying for peace of mind and the ever-watchful eye of the Lord to ensure their protection.

Then there was the matter of Stacey's pills. She'd asked her mother to give them to Maurice for safe-keeping, so that he would govern her temptation and not allow her to give in to it. Again, it was Penny who took the brunt. All attempts at negotiation on Stacey's part to get her stepfather to give in to her demands when the going got rough, were done through her mother. Without Maurice's strength of character, Penny knew she would have given in long ago as she watched her daughter suffering withdrawal.

'It's just as well she holds me in some awe,' Maurice admitted when Penny told him of the threats Stacey was making on his person at the heights—or was it the depths?—of her agonies.

At such times, Penny felt a tremendous guilt, feeling that she was inflicting all this on her new husband, feeling torn in her love for him and love for her child. Exhausted by the tensions created between all family members, with herself the central buffer for all concerned, Penny felt close to breaking point.

Inevitably, new conflicts arose out of the central issue, so that had they not been committed to regular sharing times in bed, freely communicating their anxieties and irritations with one another, Penny knew the doctor's prediction might have been well-founded. Her relationship with Maurice might well have been just one more casualty in the growing number of failed second-marriages.

It was as well she had never tried to manoeuvre Maurice into taking Stacey in. Having made known her own feelings, she had made it clear that she would respect his decision no matter what. She'd insisted that the door be left open for him to refuse. Secure in that knowledge, Penny had been free to turn to her husband, finding her own faltering strength bolstered by his quiet impartiality. By the time Stacey left home once more, lured back to her old way of life, the conflict Maurice and Penny had shared together had proved a growing point in their relationship.

With Christ Jesus the chief cornerstone, they knew the reality in their own relationship of seeing, in him, the whole building joined together and rising to become a holy temple in the Lord—a dwelling in which God lives by his Spirit.[1]

Tracing the source of the problem

The incident Penny and Maurice had experienced reminded me of a letter I had received from my closest friend, Stephanie, just prior to my marriage to Paul, though it had actually been the first night of my honeymoon before I'd been able to read it. I'd sat in bed, as Paul occupied himself with his ablutions in the en suite bathroom, the tears coursing down my cheeks. Poor man was quite concerned as he emerged to see his bride so moved.

'...and I want to send you all our love,' I'd read, 'and wish you every happiness for the future. It's a big step you're taking and if I try to put myself in your place, I imagine it has taken courage and faith. There will be the inevitable problems—but then which marriage is without those? Your temptation will be to think that it's you, because knowing your striving for perfection, you are a hard task master for yourself!! However, if there is one thing that Michael has taught me it's always to talk things out—and he's insisted on this even when I've been really obstinate! And the one thing that the Lord has taught me, is to be ready to say 'sorry' even when I'm quite convinced that it wasn't my fault. If you could be here, you would hear me laughing—Michael will tell you that it's never my fault—or so I say!

'Seriously though, I know that I can't pray—at least I can pray, but God can't hear me, if I haven't said sorry, so I'm on a losing wicket all the way round!

'I've just thought that I sound like an old Granny! Forgive me, I just long that you should be really happy and accept yourself!...and I'm sure that you're going to go on proving that "God is able to keep that which I have committed unto him...."'

The point is, that like Penny and Maurice, we too had our ups and downs with my daughters in the early days and the temptation is always to think, 'this problem has arisen out of my selfishness in wanting to remarry. In forming part of a stepfamily I have created a viper's nest of problems for all those whom I love.'

Accidental, or deliberate damage?

Keeping a perspective on the whole matter can be difficult; all families have their problem situations and not all problems are stepfamily related. But it sometimes happens that they could be divorce related.

'Linda, my youngest, was stealing from the local shop,' Isobel told us. 'Both she and Tracy felt the man in the shop was overcharging so they were getting their own back. Linda felt he'd stolen from them, and that she was, therefore, in the right.' Isobel raised thin, arched eyebrows despairingly.

'She was completely unrepentant. Warren and I went down to the shop with her to discuss it. But I don't think we had control. She had. She felt she was right and that was all that mattered. We had to bring her father in eventually.'

Privately wondering if this had been Linda's intention all along—to bring her mother and father together—I paused for a moment.

'How did that make you feel Warren?' I asked aloud.

'Oh fine.' Affably Warren dismissed any suggestion that he should feel otherwise. 'It was me that 'phoned him. I felt he would carry more authority, partly because of his being their father and partly because of his job.'

Knowing Isobel's ex-husband was a policeman, that made sense. But still I wondered at Linda's motives. A similar situation had arisen some years previously in another family. The daughter in this case, also in trouble with the police for theft, showed obvious distress when her father did not turn up, as promised, at the magistrates court.

Within a fortnight she had broken her probationary sentence by committing a crime of greater seriousness— breaking and entering. And this time she was rewarded by having both natural parents making an appearance in the

Crown Court. The only thing she hadn't bargained for was the active involvement of her father's second wife.

Years later, restored to the fold once more, she admitted to her mother her secret and deep longing to bring her parents together again. Despite the fact that with both parents remarried there was not the remotest possibility of their marriage being restored, the passion of that longing had taken over in motivating and governing the daughter's behaviour.

But whatever the motives, parents have to take appropriate action. In the case of school children it may be wise to enlighten the child's teacher. A simple appointment with the class teacher, or note to the Head will suffice, and any information so divulged will be respected as being of a confidential nature. But it will give all concerned a better opportunity of monitoring the situation, especially if there is any chance that the child might be stealing at school, or being bullied by others to do so.

The stress factor

Conflict in the home can put tremendous stress upon the second marriage, and most particularly, I think, on the wife, whether or not she is a step-parent. This in no way diminishes the distress and guilt felt by stepfathers, but women are, more often than not, the hub of the home. Knock her off-centre, or dent her edges too deeply with constant battering, and everything else follows suit—just as the spokes of a wheel would be misaligned or fall out if damage befalls the hub.

With no faith to carry them through, this is particularly true of the non-Christian family. One writer, referring to what she calls the 'regenerative Triangular Family' (two parent families) points out the way in which children draw upon their mother, whilst 'she, in turn, replenishes this maternal cornucopia through her relationship with the father, who, in giving, also receives.'[2] This is all very well up to a point, but it presupposes that each has something to give in the first place. Diminish or deny those resources at any one point by removing one parent, and the whole 'regenerative' process dries up.

If we're honest, there are times when we have all turned in upon ourselves, too overwhelmed with the problems and hurts at hand to have anything to give or be drawn upon by others. This, in turn, denies the need of children and spouse, so that they too are in danger of 'drying up'. What began as an inability to cope with the constant battering, can fast deteriorate into clinical depression. I know, I've been there during my first marriage. Yes, even as a Christian.

But when my own faith was too weak to sustain me, the prayers and support of Christian friends gradually became the medication which was to bring me up out of the downward spiral. At a time when most of my divorced friends were still on a diet of tranquillisers and sleeping pills, which only masked the problems rather than resolved them, I was lifted in the arms of the Almighty, sheltered under his wings,[3] and gradually enabled to lift up my head once more.[4]

Barrie and Margot, as non-Christians at the time of their second marriage, found it difficult to cope with the problems encountered in their stepfamily, so much so that it affected Margot's health. Margot's two daughters were only six and four years old, whilst Barrie's son and daughter Zoe were a little older.

'Zoe was at loggerheads with me all the time,' Margot told me ruefully. 'She was the only unhappy one in the whole family. I worried more about my step-children than about my own girls.'

I smiled in sympathy. Though I had no step-children myself, it was easy to imagine how that would be so.

'I found myself constantly questioning my motives,' Margot continued.

Barrie took up the story: 'By the time Zoe was about thirteen, when we'd been married five or six years, Margot was nearly having a nervous breakdown, particularly because Zoe was still being pumped by her mother every holiday.'

There was an ongoing decline until eventually Margot felt that Zoe should go to live with her mother.

'I talked it through with her and asked her if she would like to,' Margot said.

But talking it out seemed to resolve the problems, and Zoe never did go to live with her mother.

'She's very affectionate towards Margot now,' Barrie smiled, 'she even says she loves her more than her own mother.'

The anxiety felt by Margot towards her step-children, and the way in which she was constantly examining her motives, seems to be fairly common amongst step-parents. So too, is the fear that in upsetting the step-child, the step-parent runs the risk of damaging relationships with the child's natural parent.

Paul has rarely reduced Amanda to tears and on those occasions when it has happened, she has soon bounced back. Sensing his discomfort after one such incident, I asked him to describe how he felt.

'Rather a cad, really,' he replied. 'It makes me feel very insecure wondering if you will be angry, and whether it will irreparably damage my relationship with her. If that happened, I'm not sure how you would react.'

Effecting repairs

The step-parent, especially if previously unmarried, may find it incredibly difficult to say sorry to the step-child when the occasion demands. This is particularly true of a

stepfather to step-daughter. In the first instance, it may
simply be a matter of getting used to something which
seldom occurred when living alone. But in the second
situation, it may be a question of gender, whereby a
stepfather may find it infra dig as a grown man to have to
'humble himself' to a 'mere girl'. But inevitably, just as in
the natural family, there will be times when through tiredness, irritability, or an error in judgement, mistakes are
made and children treated unjustly.

Far from diminishing the stature of a stepfather, the
ability to apologise is a sign of maturity, of being 'big
enough' to acknowledge one's faults and admit to one's
human fallibility. Properly executed, a sincere apology on
the part of the step-parent (or indeed parent), can be a
most rewarding and conciliatory experience for both adult
and child.

Though there was no one incident in Margot's dealings
with Barrie's son, she has now been able to look back and
acknowledge her own human failings when things began
to go wrong with him soon after their marriage when he
was only eleven years old.

'I realise now that Tim needed a mother when Barrie
and I married,' she confessed, 'but at the time I couldn't
see that. Because my two girls were so little, he seemed so
big in comparison. I thought he was grown up. I can see
now, he wasn't.'

Because Tim was so much older, he was less malleable
than the other children, less able to be influenced, and he
had the most problems.

'Eventually, when he was sixteen, he just walked out,'
Barrie said. 'First he got a cottage, then later he went to
London.'

Margot turned to him. 'He didn't really walk out,' she
demurred mildly, 'he just sort of drifted out with our
permission.' Turning back to me, she continued: 'Actually, I felt very relieved when he left because he'd been

such a problem. But about this time, we became Christians anyway.'

Barrie nodded in agreement. 'Yes, our faith really helped us through then.'

With the flow of grace into their lives as a healing salve, Barrie and Margot were enabled to start making repairs in the damaged family relationships.

Space to manoeuvre

One of the hardest things in any family is knowing when to let go. Even in the happiest and most secure of families, the average adolescent can be a disruptive influence as the struggle to throw off the shackles of childhood and emerge an independent adult causes havoc all around. In the stepfamily, the effect can be catastrophic. Here, the 'normal' guilt which may be experienced in easing the fledgeling out of the nest is compounded by other factors.

The guilt is three-way on the part of the step-parent: toward the child, toward the child's natural parent (the step-parent's spouse), and toward 'others'—those in the wider family and outside world. As well as suspecting one's own motives, there is the constant fear of being under the secret condemnation of those 'others', and the not so secret accusation of one's nearest and dearest.

In the early months of their marriage, Doreen and Jeff experienced many problems with Jeff's son stealing. They were unable to leave any money about and tension in the family ran high. Eventually, after coming and going for a while, the boy moved out into lodgings.

Doreen nursed a terrible guilt, feeling that in some indefinable way she was responsible. Jeff wept openly when the boy finally went, which only added to his wife's feeling of guilt as she tried to comfort him.

'I felt all the time that it was their home—Jeff's and his

childrens'—and that I was an intruder,' she admitted
sadly.

But the fact is we all need space, parents, step-parents
and offspring alike. Both John White's excellent book
Parents In Pain[5] and James Dobson's equally excellent *Love
Must Be Tough*[6] spell out the principles of 'letting go'. Far
from being a matter for condemnation, it is actually Scriptural to do so at the right time.

The earliest reference to one of the prerequisites for
marriage comes in Genesis, where it speaks of 'leaving'
and 'cleaving'. Before any young man can be ready to
enter into so serious a relationship, he needs to be able to
stand on his own two feet. That means an independence—
emotionally, spiritually, and almost certainly physically,
since the first two would be difficult to achieve whilst still
under the parental roof.

When God the Father 'gave away' the bride Eve to the
bridegroom Adam, he made it clear that this was to be:
'For this reason a man will leave his father and mother
and be united to his wife, and they will become one flesh.'[7]

I'm not so sure, despite present trends, that this applies
so stringently to young women whose make up is different.
The very fact that they are 'given away' by their fathers
implies that that is the moment of 'leaving'. In any case,
many girls maintain emotional links with their parents even
after physically leaving home. Marriage demands a certain
dependence in them, and too great a degree of all-round
independence could create problems in their future relationships with the opposite sex. In this context, the Biblical
reference seems to differentiate, the term 'man' seeming to
apply to the male of the species rather than to 'mankind'.

Joint support

To be effective, when making joints in plumbing terms,
each section must be sound enough to support the other in

order that the connection may be durable. The same is true of married partners facing problems—each must be able to support the other in times of trouble in order that the marriage may survive. In other words, the problems of one partner (or parent) are the problems of the other, and need to be faced together.

It may sound elementary to state so obvious a truth. Yet it is amazing how often, when counselling, one encounters the metaphoric shrug of the shoulders indicating that either husband or wife believes the other's problems to be exclusively their own. 'That's his/her problem,' they say with deep sadness. But it isn't! A married couple are one flesh. Whatever affects one, affects the other. Inevitably.

The step-parent may be more reluctant than most to become enmeshed in parent/child relationships which he (she) feels are outside his (her) domain. But the mutual support of your partner need not be pragmatic, at least not overtly so. Indeed, it may do more harm than good for the step-parent to enter into heated discussions regarding a break-down in relationships between parent and adolescent, though this may well be a possibility with younger children. But that is not to say that discussion of a private nature between both partners should not be entered into.

A temporary clash between Penny and her eldest daughter Annabel was a case in point. It was of a temporary nature—they normally got on well together—caused by numerous outside tensions and exacerbated by the fact that Annabel was a young woman who had lived away from home, and had her own ideas as to how a home should be run now that she was back living under Penny and Maurice's roof. Considerable friction ensued for a while between the two women.

But Penny was able to receive all the support she needed from Maurice without his ever becoming embroiled. This took the form of prayer, a listening ear, wise counsel in putting across her daughter's point of view as an adult living with her natural parent and step-parent— a position Maurice had once been in—and his love and affection.

From time to time, he would 'sit in' as Penny and her daughter tried to iron out their differences. Only if asked, by one or other, or if he himself requested permission to do so, would he make any contribution. His step-daughter never had any feeling of intrusion on his part. Being emotionally distanced from the situation, he was able to view it more objectively than either mother or daughter, and although he never let his wife down in any way, he was scrupulously fair in his advice. Anything which he felt might undermine Penny's position in any way, he reserved for mention when they were alone.

But not all men are blessed with the insight of having been both step-child and stepfather. Doreen was heart-broken when her daughter Kirstin's lifestyle went right against Christian principles. Unable to understand the depth of her emotions, Jeff felt Doreen was being moody. His first wife had been a very moody person and so he took it that Doreen was turning out to be the same.

Because he was unable to cope, he did not have it in him to comfort Doreen. The only way he could deal with the situation was to shut it out, and that meant shutting his wife out too. Things became more and more strained between them, until one day the pent-up emotions of each erupted in an almighty row.

Amy, Doreen's other daughter, happened to be around at the time. A Christian herself, she made her mother and stepfather sit down and talk it all out. It was the best thing that could have happened, bringing a new understanding and commitment into their relationship. All the old hurts and misunderstandings were brought out into the open and cleared up once and for all.

'Everything came to a head when I was unhappy and

Jeff thought I was being moody,' Doreen laughed happily. 'He thought I was being like his first wife, but I'm me, not her.'

At the end of the day, we have to let our children go—at liberty to make their own decisions, free to make their own mistakes. As the Father allows us free choice, so too, must we do likewise with them, trusting that one day we shall be killing the fatted calf and rejoicing as the father did on the return of the Prodigal Son. But as Christians, this letting go is not a sign of defeat. We have the ultimate weapon—prayer.

It is within our power as parents to take authority in the name of Jesus, cutting off our children from the effects of our mistakes in their upbringing, and praying a healing into their lives. Long ago, when still in the aftermath of my divorce, I began doing just this on behalf of my daughters, praying Jesus 'in' to their lives and asking that he be a bridge between all the harmful and damaging effects of the circumstances surrounding their family life, and the abundant riches of his mercy and blessing.

Laying claim to God's promise to 'make all things work together for good'[8], I asked that they might grow up into mature and whole beings, enriched and rounded because of their experiences rather than wounded and downbeaten as one might expect.

I remember a speaker once saying that when she asked after the health of one particular acquaintance, she invariably received the reply, 'Not so bad under the circumstances'. 'What are you doing there?' she would ask. 'Jesus, has made his enemies his footstool, and since he is in us and we are in him, they become our footstool too. And where does a footstool go? Why, under our feet. So that puts us on top.'

As Christian parents, we can rise above the circumstances. For the fact is that problems, all problems, exist in people not in circumstances. It is my inability to cope with those circumstances which creates the 'problem', not the circumstances themselves.

But circumstances don't just happen in a vacuum. They 'happen' to us. They affect the choices open to me. And only because of those choices, and which of them I elect to take, do they have any bearing upon the course of my life.

God is a Father. The Father. He knows a parent's love with a fulness we shall never attain to. Whatever good and wholesome thing we want for our children, he wants it more. And he has the power to bring it about. The way we, weak and helpless, lay hold of that power to make it operative in the lives of our wayward children, is through prayer; prayer that God may complete his work in us, his children, to enable us to make the right choices.

Conflict can then become, not a destructive force, but an area for real growth. For as the Father deals with us, producing in us the fruit of the Spirit—self-discipline—so we too, may know wisdom in the disciplining of our children.

Notes

[1] From Ephesians 2:20–22
[2] Diana Davenport, *One Parent Families* (Pan Books Ltd: London).
[3] Psalm 57
[4] Psalm 3
[5] John White, *Parents In Pain* (Inter Varsity Press: Leicester, 1980).
[6] James Dobson, *Love Must Be Tough* (Kingsway: Eastbourne, 1984).
[7] Genesis 2:24
[8] Romans 8:28

9

Penalty Clauses—Discipline

It was difficult to remember afterwards—after all the commotion was over—just what had brought it to Penny's attention, and where she had been at the time. She thought she might have been upstairs, putting some ironing in the airing cupboard when the raised voices from the lounge had intruded upon her mind. By the time she had hastened downstairs Maurice and Melony, both red-faced, were confronting one another in angry silence.

'What's the problem?' Penny asked tentatively, aware that she must tread softly.

An angry cacophony exploded from the two warring members of the family. Inwardly she sighed. It was all so difficult. Not that there had been many upsets like this. Thankfully they'd been very rare. But you had to be so careful in this sort of situation not to sound as if you were behaving like a mother to your husband. Once or twice before, Melony had seemed to think that she, Penny, wielded the same maternal authority over Maurice as over herself. 'Tell him, Mum.' she'd exhorted, 'tell him he can't do that.' On another occasion, she'd gone direct to Maurice. 'Mummy says we mustn't do that!'

Penny looked from one to the other, since both had now lapsed into silence once more.

'I was in the middle of watching the news...' Maurice began, tight-lipped.

'I didn't even know he was watching...' Mel burst out passionately.

'You didn't even ask...'

The row showed signs of heating up again. Piecing together the disjointed phrases, Penny thought she could make some sense of the situation.

'You should ask, Mel, before switching over,' she said, her voice mildly reproachful.

'Well, it's our television, not his!' With tears streaming down her face, Mel slammed out of the room and pounded up the stairs to her bedroom. Her door banged shut.

Through the thin floors the sounds of her sobs were clearly audible. It was all Penny could do not to weep herself. Or to lash out at Maurice for 'upsetting' her daughter. A barrier began to be erected between all members of the family—a barrier of silent accusation and guilt.

Justifiable though Maurice's anger undoubtedly was, Penny was astute enough to realise how hurtful it must be to Melony to have your mother take sides against you. At such times, despite the affection which was so obviously growing between stepfather and child, it was easy to see that Mel perceived this man in her life as an interloper, someone who, however unintentionally, had come between her and her mother.

But to let Melony get away with such behaviour was unthinkable. Penny knew her first loyalties had to be towards her new husband. And, for her own sake as much as theirs, Mel had to understand that. She had to know that there was an unassailable unity between husband and wife.

Penny had no way of knowing exactly what had happened, but whatever the truth of the matter, it certainly wouldn't do for Mel to think that she could ride roughshod over her stepfather's wishes. Nor, however genuine her tears—and Penny knew she was not a manipulative child—that she could win her mother over to take sides against Maurice. That would be the beginning of the end. Mel had to make her apologies to her stepfather and to understand that such high-handed behaviour was unacceptable to her mother.

But Melony needed to know, nevertheless, that Penny understood. And that although she would not countenance such behaviour from her daughter, neither was there any question of her having rejected or abandoned her. She had to convey to Mel that her love for her had not diminished in any way since her marriage to Maurice.

Comforting her and explaining all this later, all barriers down, Penny felt, as she prayed with Melony, that God had used this situation for good and for growth: that through it he'd been able to bring her daughter to a new understanding—an enlarging of her perception of life. And that had included an understanding of Maurice's personal commitment to the family—spiritual, emotional and material.

At the same time, Penny knew that, in private with Maurice, she owed it to her daughter to present her side of the case, just to help him understand Melony's feelings. Wives and mothers are called to be peace-makers, she reflected later, often having to subjugate their own feelings in order to pour oil on the troubled waters of family life. Idly, she wondered how you coped without a Father on whom to off-load...?

As it happened, when she broached the subject with Maurice later that night, with their arms around each other in bed, he had already reached the same conclusions concerning Melony.

'Personally, I think she quite deliberately turned the TV over, knowing I was watching the news, but I'm prepared to give her the benefit of the doubt,' he said. 'I think she still sometimes finds my relationship with you threatening. And I can understand that.'

'Well, we're all subject to moods from time to time,' Penny smiled, grateful for his insight. 'If it was deliberate, perhaps something earlier in the day had unsettled her security and triggered a need in her to lash out and punish the only 'suitable' person available—you. The original feeling of insecurity may not even have been anything to do with you—perhaps something that happened at school.'

Maurice was silent for a while. 'I do sometimes wonder...' he began.

'What? You don't have any doubts about us do you?' Penny was concerned.

'Of course not... But...' Momentarily unable to express his feelings, he trailed off.

'You know, darling, rows like this can happen even in natural families.' Penny refused to use the term 'normal' families, but one had to differentiate sometimes. 'If Mel and I had been living alone and something had happened at school to unsettle her, she'd have taken it out on me. That's happened before.'

Anxiously she encouraged Maurice to face the facts. 'And it's just as likely to have happened with a natural father as with a stepfather,' she continued. 'I think it's a great mistake to imagine that all the ills that befall one can be traced directly back to the fact of being a stepfamily. You can just become paranoid about everything if you go too far down that track.'

Being the boss

Penny and Maurice's experience highlights the problems felt by many stepfamilies when it comes to the day-to-day disciplining of children. The Bible quite clearly puts the business of disciplining squarely on the father's shoulders — a natural turn of events in the Jewish patriarchal society of the times. These were the attitudes prevailing also in our own culture until recently when men have seemingly abdicated from these responsibilities, helped, no doubt, by the feminist movement which has so undermined the role of men in general and husbands/fathers in particular.

Not that one would advocate a return to the heavy-handed disciplinarians of the Victorian era. These too, are anathema to what God has to say on the matter.

'Fathers, do not exasperate your children; instead, bring them up in the training and instruction of the Lord.'[1]

But where does this leave the stepfather? Paul and I have witnessed the devastating effect which hasty, thoughtless authoritarianism can have on the relationship between step-child and step-parent.

'Your table manners are appalling,' one very new second-husband rebuked his wife's daughter. 'Take your elbows off the table.'

'You're not my real father,' the child spat venomously. 'You've no right to tell me what to do.'

How right she was under the circumstances and in the light of the previous scripture, though no one could condone her behaviour. For although authority is a status endowed upon parents, respect has to be earned. And where the natural parent has had years in which to win the esteem of his/her children (or not, in which case he/she has only him/herself to blame), the step-parent is at a distinct disadvantage. Already, perhaps, resented for their 'intrusion' upon the family unit, it will take time and effort before the children can be won over, so that a good working relationship, built on mutual respect and affection, can be established.

To come right in and rest upon the 'authority' of adulthood, without regard to the child's feelings, could forever destroy any hope of nurturing that respect and affection so essential to the well-being of the family. Whilst a teacher or headmaster may wield an authority of a different nature, the child's only experience of family authority, prior to the second marriage, will have come from its parents. Theirs has been the prerogative to reprimand, punish or withhold favours. For the step-parent to attempt to step straight into the shoes of the absent parent will be seen as one more attempt at usurpation.

Happiness equals harmony

The natural parent has a further advantage over the step-parent. Punishment can be balanced by affection. A child chastised by her mother, has, one would hope, the experience of years of loving care to weigh against the punishment of the moment. Though most children will express hate towards their parents at the height of the conflict, it is the hate of having their own will thwarted, rather than a genuine hatred against the person of their mother or father. A very real resentment of the step-parent, however, can easily develop into a very real hatred.

However, this is not always the case. As one family clearly demonstrated, the situation can be reversed with the children receiving a greater demonstration of affection from the step-parent than from the natural parent, though not always with the desired effect.

'Discipline is still, to some degree, a problem,' one stepfather told us, a year or so after his second marriage. 'Olivia was about ten or eleven when her mother and I married. She'd taken over the role of the "other partner" when her father left and she was obviously resentful of my taking the head of the table, or saying certain things.'

Sandra nodded. 'Olivia took over as the helper at mealtimes. As there were four of us, there was a side of the table for everyone. But when Peter came, she had to be moved. She felt she was being pushed out in more ways than one. She tells me now she thought he was going to steal me away.'

'To begin with, if I showed any affection to Sandra, she used to say things like "Take your arm off my mummy. She's *my* mummy," ' Peter affirmed. 'I thought: how can we deal with this without her feeling we're taking everything away? It affected the relationship between Sandra and I for a while because every time I tried to assert an air of authority, there was a kick-back from Olivia and it upset Sandra.'

A powerfully built man, Peter is nevertheless, of his own admission, nothing more than a big kid at heart. Sandra's girls had never known the freedom of demonstrative affection from their father, and it didn't take long before they warmed to their stepfather's obvious love of children.

'As the eldest, it took Olivia longer than the twins,' Sandra smiled, 'but they saw Peter loved them and they responded to that love.'

'Unfortunately, after the initial rejection of my authority, Olivia over-responded,' Peter told us frankly. 'She'd missed out on the normal pre-puberty relationship with her father, and it was as if she hadn't had chocolate cake before and now wanted to gorge herself. She hung all over me. It got embarrassing for everyone.'

'We had to explain to her that she was growing up...,' Sandra began. 'Rather than reject her for being all over Peter when we came home from work, he used to turn her to me and say "Go and give your mum a cuddle first." She'd cooled down a bit then by the time she got back to Peter.'

'We had to discipline by changing the emphasis,' Peter said thoughtfully, as he cast his mind back. 'Olivia was the eldest daughter and we had to play on that—appealing to her sense of wanting to be grown-up.'

The children in Isobel and Warren's family also

responded well to their stepfather's affection and sense of fun, with the added advantage that they were younger than Sandra's three. When it comes to authority it seems that the younger the child, the easier the task before the step-parent.

'I think I've behaved as a normal parent would,' Warren told us in response to our questioning. 'If they've needed discipline, I've disciplined them. But then I don't mind looking an idiot, messing around, having fun, so it balances out.'

Paul and I had witnessed Warren's rough and tumble with Isobel's girls and it was very evident that they thoroughly enjoyed his 'he-man' approach and easy charm. But despite the years of affection he has had to build upon, he nevertheless ran into trouble as the girls approached adolescence.

Simon's family were younger still, with the roles reversed, but their stepmother, Ros, coped equally well. A sensible young woman, she recognises that not all problems are the result of being a stepfamily, and that the perennial conflicts have to be tackled jointly, just as in any family.

'Kevin only tolerates church now he's older,' Simon admitted. 'But we don't push it.'

'No, but until he's sixteen, we shall encourage him to keep going,' Ros agreed.

'We'd insist until then,' Simon corrected her, 'but you can't be too heavy. I head up some of the meetings and you can see him cringe. He must be sitting there thinking to himself, "Now what's he up to?" They get easily embarrassed in their teens.'

Judging from our own situation, Paul feels that much of the success in disciplining is directly attributable to the relationship generally, and that this, in turn, is largely dependent on the child's relationship with the natural parent. He feels that where there is love and harmony between parent and child, the child will want to please that parent. One obvious way to do so is also to please the step-parent, since to disobey or rebel against the step-parent will incur the wrath of the parent.

He balances that premise, however, with the supposition that there may well be instances when a child does not get on with the natural parent, and may find an ally in the step-parent. To some extent this may be true. We have learned of several families where the children have found it easier to confide in the step-parent than in the natural parent, but this has usually been in respect of events pertaining to the absent parent, or the divorce or death of that parent, which might cause the natural parent pain. For myself, I feel it would be a rare breed of step-parent who could, without any disloyalty to their spouse, be an ally of a rebellious child.

United we stand

As with decision-making, it may be necessary for the natural parent to have to 'set-up' the step-parent as head of the family when it comes to discipline. Just as Penny had to relay Maurice's decision regarding Stacey's smoking, so too, she had to see it through, adhering to his policy whatever the pressure put upon her by her daughter. Whilst great sensitivity must be shown in order not to alienate one's children by seeming to take sides against them, a united front between parent and step-parent is essential. Warren and Isobel confessed to their problems in this respect.

'If there was any problem in my disciplining the kids,' Warren told us, 'it was with Isobel having to take a back seat.' He smiled broadly in the direction of his wife. 'You see, she didn't always agree with what I did.'

Isobel raised her eyes in mock exasperation. 'I've never disagreed with you in front of the children,' she said. Then addressing me: 'I don't think Warren always thinks a punishment through. Going to bed at 6 pm every night for a fortnight puts tremendous strain on all the family.'

Warren laughed good-naturedly. 'Yes, that's one of my faults. I tend to stick to what I've decided and won't back down.'

'Has it ever back-fired on you?' I asked with amusement.

'Not really. Once when Tracy was going on about her father I said, "Right! If he's so terrific go and live with him." She was really shocked because she knew I meant it. So I dialled the number and she spoke to him.'

'Her father was just as shocked to think he might have to have her,' Isobel laughed.

'So you went along with it all?' I asked her.

'Oh yes. I was a part of it as it was happening. Life was unbearable with Tracy. But things got better by the minute because she knew we would have carried out our threat.'

Peter and Sandra too, feel that they each balance out the other's approach to disciplining, though they don't always see eye to eye, as Sandra told us.

'I find it very difficult sometimes having three children during the week and running my business, then when it gets to the weekend having to cope with six children. Once a fortnight we have three of Peter's four to stay over-night—his eldest is grown-up and has her own flat.

'One night Lucy, Peter's youngest, was crying because she'd hurt herself—hours before mind you. I couldn't do anything with her and when her crying set her sister off, I sent Peter up to deal with them. Lucy kept saying she wanted to go home. I felt Peter should have put his foot down, and that he'd spent far too long pandering to them...'

'My son, Robert was downstairs with Olivia.' Peter took up the story, 'And the four of us prayed. We made it clear to them that it was *our* decision, we didn't try to involve them in the conflict, but Rob is very mature; he knew the girls and how they behave at home with their mother and he said they were just trying to play us up.'

'Though I felt put out with Peter,' Sandra admitted, 'it was a difficult situation. Either way we couldn't win — his ex-wife would have used it against us if we took the girls home, or if we kept them and didn't give in to their distress. As it was they went to sleep and apologised in the morning. But I felt Peter didn't handle it well.'

'To put the other side of the coin though,' Peter defended himself, 'Sandra sometimes has a short fuse. It takes a while before she gets worked up, but when she does, she goes totally.' He grinned at his wife who nodded in agreement. 'That has created problems between us,' he continued. 'In the same way I've sometimes resented her stepping in and telling me I'm not firm enough, she some-times resents my saying she's too hard.'

'But thinking about it, we do balance each other out,' Sandra encouraged him.

Averting an all-out strike

No child will learn to respect an adult who does not stand up for himself. This is particularly true of the teenager. At the stage where the youngster is trying hard to shake off the shackles of parenthood and emerge into adulthood himself, there is a potential battlefield over every issue.

Selfishness and self-centredness epitomise this struggle for supremacy. But for parent and step-parent alike, it helps to cast your mind back to your own evolutionary process. Selfishness is often only thoughtlessness, brought on by the myriad attractions beckoning in the world around, and self-centredness the paradoxically over-whelming joy and delight in the wonder of their emerging God-created personality along with their 'despairingly hopeless, desperately depressing' inability to live up to their self-imposed expectations.

But understanding their situation is no reason to back down on every issue. The policy of the household should be stated clearly and simply, be it the hours of curfew, drinking and driving, mealtimes or household chores, and then adhered to at all times. Everyone then knows where they stand. Exceptions can be made where appropriate, provided it is clearly impressed upon the youngster that a concession is being made and that this does not set a precedent for future policy.

Doreen, already the mother of one teenaged daughter and another in her twenties, became stepmother to Jeff's teenagers when she remarried. After years of coping alone, Jeff held quite strong views when it came to the discipline of his adolescents.

'I told Doreen she must put her foot down and not let them get away with anything,' he admitted.

Doreen smiled diffidently. 'I feel I must go gently and not sort of boss Kirstin, because this is her home.'

Jeff felt his daughter didn't do enough around the house and was quite put out with all that Doreen did for her.

'I even do Kirstin's washing and ironing,' Doreen admitted, 'which I didn't do for my own daughters. But I just feel sorry for Kirstin because of the years she had no mother. I suppose I want to make it up to her, though sometimes I do feel a bit put upon.'

Stepfathers too can find teenagers bring their own set of problems. Paul, used to a small telephone bill commensurate with his bachelor lifestyle, found it difficult, to say the least, to come to terms with the much higher figure run up by the family.

'As a bachelor I knew exactly where I stood,' he admitted. 'There was only me to consider, and when I went off to work there was no one at home to be running up bills of any sort—heating, lighting or telephone. I was in complete control. It's hard coming to terms with the fact that other people — your step-children — have a call on your money and that they're spending it while you're actually earning it.'

Brought up in an era of careful constraint, the blasé attitudes of today's youth are an enigma to those unused to their easy-come-easy-go philosophy. But how, as a step-father, do you impose your disciplines upon the already established behaviour of the family?

'With difficulty,' Paul smiled wryly.

In all honesty, it was usually I who had to convey to the girls Paul's desire for restraint in the use of the telephone, and we were fortunate in that, though it had never occurred to her to do so when her father and I were together, Susie willingly offered to pay a proportion of the bill when it came in, understanding immediately the invidiousness of Paul's position. Eventually, the two were able to work out Susie's commitment without further pre-amble on my part.

Another couple with a daughter in her early twenties found her propensity to pick up undesirable boyfriends in the local pubs, and then invite them in for coffee after they had brought her home in the early hours of the morning, gave them endless sleepless nights.

'I feel as if they're "casing the joint",' her stepfather confessed, 'and that one day we'll come home from work to find everything gone.'

Because of immense problems in the girl's past, neither mother nor stepfather felt able to raise the issue, and simply learned to live with the problem and the tensions it created.

Putting all hands to the wheel

When it comes to general rules about disciplining, there can be few finer authorities than James Dobson and his excellent books on the subject. Isobel and Warren read extensively to further their understanding of the responsibilities of parenthood and the most productive methods of shaping the lives of the children in their care. But when all is said and done, there will always be the black sheep who, no matter how attentive to detail their parents may be, simply will not or cannot respond in the correct way.

It is vital to realise that this happens in all families, and that even in the most stable of environments, with loving, caring parents and an absence of any degree of trauma, one child or more may go 'off the rails'. But the fact that there have been 'rails' in the first place is sufficient to give the parents hope that the child will return.

'Train a child in the way he should go,' says the Proverb, 'and when he is old he will not turn from it.'[2]

The story of the Prodigal Son is the enactment of that wise adage.

Amongst 'normal, happy and stable' two-parent Christian families we know of problems with the children including habitual drunkenness, convictions for drunken driving, drug addiction, incest, rape, teenage pregnancies and unmarried mothers, abortion and theft. All were less than twenty years of age.

To our knowledge, those same problems exist in no greater proportion amongst stepfamilies. All we can do as adults, whether parents, step-parents, grandparents or any other caring and influential person, is to do our best— to be prepared to admit our failings, our lack of knowledge, the deficiency of our understanding. And through prayer, reading, research, discussion and effort, be determined to learn more, to become 'experts' in the highest calling any human being can have—that of pitting our wills with the Creator in the task of guiding, shaping and the making of his creation.

Reversing the sabotage

Perhaps one way in which this might be achieved would be through a structure of Parent Support Groups whereby, under the guidance of those trained in simple psychology and childhood behaviour, parents could meet to discuss openly and honestly the problems that face them in today's society. For whilst rebellion is at the heart of all men, our children are lured by temptations undreamed of in the days of our youth. Yet why is it that we let pride—our pride—stand in the way of admitting our fears for our children? Why wait until the child's rebellion has led him into that 'far off country'?

Pride is not at stake—at least not in the sense we perceive it. It isn't a question of admitting that you've failed as a parent. Society is the enemy—the society of laissez-faire, of greed, of apathy, of lustful and voracious appetites for 'more' and 'better' and 'bigger', for greater and wider experiences, each serving not to slake the thirst but to whet the appetite still further. That society is the society we have created, through our demands as much as through our inactivity. To that extent we are responsible. To that extent pride is on the line.

Attempting to discipline our children is like snipping at the top growth of a fast-developing thicket. Only if we cut back the roots will we see the arrest of its growth and eventual demise. The Bible tells us quite clearly that we become what we imbibe. A diet of TV sex and violence, blatant consumerism and avarice is hardly in keeping with the true, noble, right, pure, lovely, admirable, excellent and praiseworthy things which should occupy our minds and fill our lives.[3] Yet how can we justify a discipline which says, 'Don't do as I do, do as I say?'

The dictionary definition of the verb to discipline is 'To bring under control, train to obedience and order.' Under the word disciple the following exposition is given: 'one of

Christ's personal followers...any believer in Christ; follower or adherent of any leader of thought, art, conduct.' Since the Latin *discipulus*, from the verb *discere*—to learn, is at the root of both the verb to discipline and the noun disciple, is it unreasonable to suppose that the greatest source of 'training to obedience and order' is by example? As we follow and adhere to Christ and his 'thought, art and conduct', and through the power of his Holy Spirit become changed into his likeness, may we not expect our children to learn in like fashion from our example?

Who can blame today's children, after watching us standing on our 'rights' rather than laying down our lives for others, seeking our personal happiness at the expense of those we profess to love, breaking our promises and making money and pleasure our twin gods, for following in our footsteps? The fact that we then rationalise our actions to appease our conscience only serves to show us as hypocrites to the younger generation.

Let's admit that we got it wrong in the past. That the permissiveness of the sixties with its Doctor Spock attitudes towards the undisciplined, free-expression of children hasn't worked. There may be those reading these words who are young enough to have been the children of that era, and to have been brought up with the terms self-discipline and duty a dirty word. Let's unite as parents in a common aim to pool our resources, to encourage the fruit of the Spirit in our own lives and through *self-discipline* to return to a uniformity of morals and values based on Scriptural principles.

Let's be salt and light in the world, shaking off apathy and defeatism to influence what comes through our TV screens, what toys our children play with, what magazines our teenagers read and what music they hear.[4] But let's never forget that the greatest influence of all will be through the quality of our own lives. In the words of my

Pastor and friend David Luce, 'Our lives are the world's Bible: is the print clear?'

Notes

1. Ephesians 6:4
2. Proverbs 22:6
3. Philippians 4:8
4. Not as idealistic as it may sound: numerous organisations seek the support of Christians in turning the tide of degeneration in the fabric of society—the family unit. Listed below are the names and addresses of campaigns you could become involved with. Newsletters will keep you informed.

   Care Campaign, 21a Down Street, London W1Y 7DN—they have just launched a new magazine 'Care For The Family'. Deals with such issues as abortion, childlessness, child-abuse.

   Familybase, Jubilee House, 3 Hooper Street, Cambridge, CB1 2NZ—launched by Jubilee Trust. Deals with such issues as debt, longer pub hours.

   Media Awareness Project, Mary Sumner House, 24 Tufton Street, London SW1P 3RB—launched by The Jerusalem Trust. As its title denotes, deals with radio, TV and newspapers and how we can influence them.

   Christian Family Magazine, 37 Elm Road, New Malden, Surrey KT3 3HB—available from Christian bookshops. Seeks to explore the problems confronting families today and sometimes runs campaigns against such things as The Dungeons in London and various occult toys for young children, Halloween, etc.

   Intercessors For Britain, 14 Orchard Road, Moreton, Wirral, Merseyside, L46 8TS—cell groups for intercessory prayer. Produces a bi-monthly newsheet giving up-to-date news on issues affecting society, sometimes on a political level, i.e. religious observance in schools.

   Scripture Union, 130 City Road, London EC1V 2NJ, has a

quarterly magazine called Outreach and is active in minis-
tries in schools, families and amongst young people.
Resources packs are available to help parents become
involved.

10

Entrances and Exits

'It's no good,' Maurice regarded Penny gravely over the top of the newspaper. 'You'll have to speak to her, reassure her, tell her there's no sense of competition between her father and me.'

Penny nodded. Reluctantly she had to agree that all was not well, that Melony, every time she went to stay with her father, returned home with a vendetta against Maurice. Not that Richard often availed himself of the 'reasonable access' granted to him by the courts. More often than not it was the girls who telephoned him, instigating some meeting or other. But for all the subdued excitement on Mel's part at the prospect of seeing her father, there was always this underlying tension on her return. Highly volatile—in complete contrast to her usual phlegmatic self—she picked unprovoked quarrels with Maurice for days after and was easily moved to tears.

'I can't understand it,' Penny remarked in response to Maurice. 'I mean, she gets on so well with you.'

'It's probably a question of loyalties.' With his own stepfamily background, plus a wealth of experience in the classroom, Maurice was able to see beyond his step-daughter's often hurtful and bizarre behaviour.

Annabel too, when Penny raised the subject with her,

perceived the confusion and insecurity at the base of her younger sister's moods.

'She gets on so well with Maurice now, I think she expects to have the same sort of relationship with Dad, and when she doesn't, because she sees so little of him they're like strangers to each other, she feels let down and takes it out on Maurice.'

Penny pursed her lips. 'You may be right,' she nodded slowly. 'I wonder if she feels guilty too, because she gets on better with Maurice than with your father?'

Choosing a time when she could talk uninterrupted with Melony, Penny opened up the subject.

'Do you know why you feel so disgruntled with Maurice when you come back from seeing Daddy?' she asked gently.

Melony shrugged. It was obvious that she was as bewildered with her irrational behaviour as were the rest of the family.

'Do you feel that if you love Maurice, there won't be enough love left over for Daddy?' Penny persisted.

Melony nodded tearfully.

'Well, love isn't like a cake,' Penny explained, taking her daughter's hands in her own as they sat in the bedroom. 'If you cut a slice out for one person, that doesn't mean that there's less left for everyone else. Don't you remember the song you used to sing in Junior School?' Softly, liltingly, Penny began to sing:

> Love is something if you give it away,
> Give it away, give it away
> Love is something if you give it away,
> You keep on getting more.

'You see love grows. The more that's needed and the more people there are to share it out to, the more love expands. Maurice isn't competing with Daddy. You don't have to feel guilty, as if enjoying being with Maurice deprives Daddy in any way. They're two different people and you can love them both, and have different relationships with both without detracting from either one.'

It was incredible, Penny thought looking back months later, what that simple explanation and the prayer that had followed had done in setting Mel free. If ever there had been an instant answer to prayer, that was it. As she'd watched the instantaneous, liberalising effect on Mel's behaviour, Penny marvelled at the gentle work of the Holy Spirit in bringing wholeness into the life of one of God's children; in destroying the 'concrete cancer' of condemnation which had threatened to consume the fabric of all that was potentially good in Mel's ability to relate to others. From that day on, only the normal ups and downs of family life had prevailed, their root in the hurts of the past having been severed.

Creaky hinges

This whole area of access is fraught with problems for most families split by the trauma of divorce, and is usually compounded in stepfamilies. Complications arise simply through the inclusion of other family members, their personalities, preferences and opinions. Loyalties are stretched to the limit when they have to spread over so large an area. Step-parent must consider spouse, and spouse step-parent; both must be sensitive to the rights of the absent parent, the desires of the children, the needs of the step-children. Grandparents, past and present (though they can never truly be 'past') with their feelings and need to be included, create further tensions in the already over extended and time consuming demands made upon the limited resources of the family unit, already under siege from 20th Century society.

Numerous families testified to the problems facing them in this area, many expressing the feeling that in this

respect, bereavement must be easier to cope with. Roles
are more clearly defined, loyalties less divided, and rejection less of a problem. For many parents the possibility of
access is greater than they wish to avail themselves of; for
most children, access to the absent parent doesn't occur
often enough.

'Their father has access whenever he wants,' Isobel told
us. 'But it's never as often as the children want.'

Warren nodded. 'Invariably, it's when they contact
him.'

'He only rings when it suits.' Isobel shrugged.

'If they waited for him,' Warren agreed, 'he wouldn't
contact them at all.'

Several families felt that the absent parent made no
allowances for the fact that the children, and the stepfamily in which they lived, had an ongoing life, with
events planned and family arrangements made. It seemed
to be outside their scope of thinking, as if, because they no
longer had a daily involvement with their children, they
believed them to be living in a vacuum, awaiting a call to
arrange access. Isobel confirmed this:

'He'll say, "You can come this weekend" and then
Tracy will say, "I've got a disco".'

If inflexible attitudes are held, tensions are set up in the
family: the absent parent may believe that the custodial
parent is being deliberately awkward when the child produces a previously made family arrangement as a reason
for being unable to visit; the child is torn by divided
loyalties and desires; and the custodial parent can end up
piggy-in-the-middle. But it can also happen in reverse.

Peter's children live with his ex-wife, and a flexible
access was agreed at the time of the divorce because it
suited both parents.

'But there was a definite resentment on the part of my
ex-wife when I had the children whilst I was courting
Sandra,' Peter recalled. 'She was afraid I would take them

to visit her. It was obvious that she said things to the girls to put them off.'

'We'd arrange to spend the weekend separately,' Sandra explained, 'and Peter's girls would keep asking him "Aren't we going to see Sandra's girls?". It just didn't tie up with what their mum was saying.'

'One weekend when the kids were coming down over-night, the youngest wanted me to take her back early on the Sunday to go to a party, and then take the other two back later.' Peter raised his eyebrows expressively. 'We said to her, "You have to choose. If you want to see us, come; if not, don't." '

Sandra nodded. 'If they've something else on, they're free not to come. We're happy.'

Peter laughed in exasperation. 'Susie came that week-end, and then got her stepfather to pick her up for the party. She used to ask what we were doing and weigh up whether it was better than what she had planned—hedg-ing both ends towards the middle!'

Further tensions are created through the quality of access in financial terms, as Isobel explained.

'The girls get very hurt about their father's lack of financial input. They work out what we spend and what he spends on them, and feel rejected by him.'

But this situation is not always the case. There are absent parents who seem to set themselves up in financial competition with the step-parent in order to curry favour with the children.

This manipulative attitude can arise in both the custodial parent and the absent parent, not only through money, but in any number of other ways, and is tremen-dously damaging to the emotional development of the child. Stress, induced when children are forced to take sides as they take the brunt of a constant verbal side-swiping, can manifest itself as speech-impediments, skin-rashes and disorders, gastric upsets, headaches and bed-wetting.

But this is only the outward sign of a potentially lethal emotional destruction. For as well as impairing their natural emotional development in that they are candidates for broken relationships in the future, their spiritual progress may also be hindered. Hardening of the heart can be as inevitable a consequence of the wrong emotional diet, as hardening of the arteries through the wrong culinary intake.

Though it may not at first sight be apparent, the insidious influence upon these children is to teach them manipulative procedures themselves. Adults coming for counselling during the break-up of their own marriage relationship, may appear, at first sight, to be utterly innocent victims. Only on closer inspection can it be seen that because of their own past history they have subtly, and almost certainly sub-consciously, applied the same emotional blackmail to their partner as was applied to them in their childhood. The result is that the partner is eventually driven away, perhaps blinded to what is happening and aware only of an inability to meet the demands made upon them.

This was potentially the situation with Simon's children when his eldest daughter wanted to live with him rather than her mother. The girl told her father that her mother had said, 'You'll be at the back of the queue.'

'I think she fosters it in the girls,' Simon said.

Barrie and Margot's situation was almost identical. Zoe, Barrie's eldest daughter, was on the receiving end from her mother. Although it was Jayne who had broken up her family home by going off with Margot's husband Jeremy, she seemed to be unable to accept the input which Margot had into Zoe's life when she and Barrie eventually married.

'Daddy won't love you any more now he's married her,' Jayne told her daughter.

Inevitably, as a youngster, Zoe's understanding of the situation was limited and initially she accepted what her mother had to say, blaming Margot for everything. Living as she did with her brother and Margot's two girls, she began, as the only step-daughter in the household, to feel more and more unhappy, her isolation and emotional turmoil exacerbated by the continual pressure to which her mother subjected her. Unable to cope, Zoe became more and more difficult to the point where Margot, not yet a Christian at this stage, nearly went under with a nervous breakdown.

It was at this point that Margot discovered that part of the problem was caused by Zoe being the only girl in the stepfamily not calling her 'Mum', due to her own mother's insistence that she should not do so. Zoe had felt an outcast, not properly one of the family, and when asked what she would like to call Margot, she admitted the truth. Between all concerned, it was agreed that in order not to hurt her own mother, it was better to keep from her the fact that Zoe was now calling her stepmother 'Mum'. In God's grace, that simple step was a turning point in the relationship between stepmother and step-daughter.

For one step-daughter, now grown up, the gulf between herself and her stepmother has, if anything, widened with the years. From the early days when the children were barely into their teens, the stepmother, believing quite falsely that a division existed in the natural family, began taking sides against them, gossiping in a slanderous way about the others whenever her step-daughter visited.

'Though I'd love to see him alone, I still can't stand going to stay with my father,' Louise told me, 'or even meeting him for a drink or a meal because Sylvia always comes—she'll never let me see him alone—and she spends the whole time running down my mother and sister. She does it in a sort of conspiratorial way, putting her arm through mine and taking me off quietly. It's just as if she thinks that because I've left home, I don't get on with my family. I think she thinks it will please me—as if she's an ally and it's she and I against my mother and sister.'

This same stepmother was, herself, a step-child. Her insecurities affect the whole family, including her second marriage. Her husband, Nick, admits that she can't bear him to see his children, even though they are now grown-up. Reading between the lines, one can't help but feel that the venom of her jealousy must cause untold tensions. Deirdre, the eldest daughter, is usually at the butt of her stepmother's poison.

'She quite literally cannot stand the sight of me,' Deirdre admitted. 'Even to my face she makes snide remarks, though she's careful never to be too hostile in front of my father. But nothing is sacred. My figure, my hairstyle, clothes, boyfriends, job, and, of course, most of all my mother; Sylvia never lets an opportunity go by without making some sort of derogatory remark.'

It may be that because of Deirdre's age and the fact that she and her father were close when he and Sylvia married, Sylvia sees her as the other woman—at best in competition with herself, at worst a threat to her relationship with Nick. Though such a notion may seem somewhat ridiculous to those in secure and loving relationships, to those already suffering from emotional insecurity it is simply a natural extension of low self-esteem.

Already bowed down with feelings of inadequacy and lack of worth, perhaps stemming from their own childhood, such people find it hard to believe that they can ever be accepted or loved. This is especially true if the stepmother was, herself, the 'other woman' instrumental in breaking up the first marriage. Not only does guilt then become a factor, but also the knowledge that where she has succeeded in the past in luring the man in question into adultery, some other woman may succeed in the future.

For the Christian, no such extremes of insecurity should exist. Secure in the knowledge of who we are in Christ—unique and beloved by the Father, moving in the power of the Spirit—and with prayer as the means of guidance to prevent us from erring, and forgiveness through the Cross should we fall, we have the means to be whole people, well able to cope with all that confronts us. When the storms of life threaten to engulf us, we can say with Paul: 'We are hard pressed on every side, but not crushed; perplexed, but not in despair; persecuted, but not abandoned; struck down, but not destroyed.'[1]

If only we realised what a privilege it is to be called to be parents. And what an awesome responsibility. It behoves us to be sensitive to the feelings of the children in our care, and to make the path smooth for them whenever possible. We hold in our hands the potential of the world to come!

'We try to be flexible with Simon's second wife seeing Kevin and Patsy.' Ros told me one day, as we sat in our lounge.

'She's no problem anyway,' Simon agreed. 'Daphne never married the father of the twins she had before she and I got married so she understands the problem from the other side. I brought the twins up as mine when we did marry, and we used to restrict their father's access for my benefit, so she realises that Ros is bringing up Kevin and Patsy and needs to know where she stands. Daphne's like a favourite aunt. All the kids' maternal needs are met in Ros.' He smiled fondly in her direction. 'You wouldn't know she wasn't their mum. Even in the negative things.'

'Kevin never says, "You're not my real mum"?' Paul asked.

'No.' Ros shook her head. 'Though I think he tried testing me recently when I was nagging. He burst into tears when I said he couldn't have any peas. But it wasn't really the peas. We sat and talked about it. I said I loved him but I wanted other people to like him and that was why I kept on top of him. It was a real step forward for me—talking to him as an adult.

'But there was an occasion when he went out with his mother and wouldn't say goodbye to her when they came home. It was as if he was trying to shield his father.' Ros's attractive face softened as she recalled. 'Dear little chap! He was only five.'

'You resented Daphne, didn't you?' Simon suddenly interjected.

'I tried to talk naturally about her so Kevin didn't feel he had to choose sides. But I found it difficult when Daphne gave them sweets and so on. But then I realised that in her position I'd be just the same. Patsy used to boast with her friends when they were saying, "I've got this or that" "I've got two mums", she'd say. That really got at me. She'd even tell strangers.'

Another couple's experience has not been so happy, as Gina relayed to us one evening over a snack. There had been an incident before she and Philip married, when the girls had been visiting their father and he had left them alone one night. As one daughter is asthmatic, it was obviously a potentially dangerous situation.

'Unlike Philip, who has joint custody of his kids, I have sole custody of my girls,' Gina told us. 'I sought guidance from other Christians after that incident. The girl my "ex" was living with had had four husbands and three lovers, so I didn't want my girls sleeping at her house, so I let them go during the day but never overnight. He used to take them to the pub for lunch.

'But it all rather backfired on me, because his present wife now says that if she wasn't good enough before, she

can't be now, so they're never allowed to stay overnight.
Because of that, there's a certain amount of venom directed at me.

'She resents me because I have the house and everything. So my "ex" doesn't always tell her everything.
Things he doesn't want her to know, he says the girls
mustn't let on about. My eldest says she doesn't see why
he should tell them what they can and can't say.'

Keeping the hinges oiled

A similar situation arose between two other women and
again highlights the insecurity felt by some second wives.
It all came out over the dinner table, when both wives
were attending the same wedding. Because the first wife
had not wanted her children to come into contact with the
second wife whilst she was simply their father's girlfriend,
the second wife had nursed a grievance in her heart for
years. Unable to accept the olive branch held out by the
first wife once she had married the children's father, her
resentment and bitterness was so obviously destroying her
own peace of mind.

'If only you would forgive her,' her dinner companion,
a close friend of mine urged her. 'You would feel such
release.'

'How can I?' the woman responded. 'You don't understand...'

'I understand that it's destroying your life, and that you
can give it all to God and know peace,' my friend replied.

It all comes down to choices. God has given us freedom
of choice. It is his will that we choose the way of Jesus—of
forgiveness and love. We can't change our emotions but
we do have control over our will. And it's in the surrender
of our will to God's will that he is able to change our
emotions.

Paradoxically, I have heard of couples who seem to

have achieved the impossible in that they have become bosom buddies with their estranged partners and their new spouses. But strangely enough, this seems to be a phenomenon of the world rather than the church. Frankly, I feel that to do so is to view the bonds of marriage so lightly as to condone the swapping of partners.

·   The fact remains that God says quite clearly, 'I hate divorce.'[2] Divorce is an evil and we are told to eschew evil.[3] How confusing it must be to the children, still nursing their hurts, to see the parents who have torn apart their security, now embracing a close social standing with each other and their new partners.

However, that is not to say that we should not reach out in the love of God and with his perception and compassion for those who are lost in darkness. But this can be done without hob-nobbing socially. Simple civility, flexibility, an understanding of the durability of the child/parent relationship despite the severance of their parents' relationship, can smooth the path of all concerned.

It was never Paul's intention to meet my 'ex'. We neither of us felt the desire to socialise with him or his second wife. But then one Christmas, as we took the girls over to exchange presents, he came out to the car and invited us in for a drink. To refuse would have been crass and churlish, and though it was hardly a carefree and relaxed meeting, I think the girls were pleased to see that we were all able to behave in a civilised manner. It has smoothed the path also, for the odd occasion when he has telephoned and spoken to Paul, sometimes asking his opinion on various problems which the girls might be going through.

Doreen too has met Jeff's ex-wife and feels that for the children's sake she must talk naturally with her. Privately, however, she finds it difficult to understand how she could have left her children.

For Warren, it has not simply been a case of meeting Isobel's ex-husband, he has actually had to deal with most of the necessary contact between the two families.

'Isobel never has any contact with her "ex",' he explained, 'because there's always been conflict between the two.'

'It arose over school fees,' Isobel went on. 'In front of the children he said he wouldn't pay for my younger daughter. It made me ill.'

Warren's face looked grim. 'I told him anything that has to be done in future, is to be done through me. And he's quite happy about that.'

Isobel nodded. 'Anything he has to discuss he discusses with Warren. Whatever Warren arranges is done—school fees, holidays...'

Caught in the revolving doors

Ros, of course, is in the invidious position of having two ex-wives to cope with, and step-children from both, one set living with their mother, the other two with herself and Simon, as well as the two she and Simon have had since their marriage. Six children in all, ranging from toddlers to upper teens.

'Every time I've had another child, the eldest feels pushed further back,' Simon confessed. 'She still comes round, even though she's eighteen, but she's been a bit difficult at times. It's been fourteen years since I lived with them as a father, but I think their mother talked about me in front of them.'

'So do you feel she's turned them against you?' I asked.

'Not consciously,' he admitted honestly. 'She's had a lot of boyfriends, her second marriage didn't work, and Brenda accused her mother of being a failure.'

'She won't run her mum down in front of us though,'

Ros interjected. 'Both children are very supportive towards her. Brenda mothers her mother.'

'She's done a good job in bringing them up,' Simon agreed generously. 'But though she's happy to take the praise when all is going well, when it goes wrong, it's my fault. Since I became a Christian, she's accused me of putting the fellowship first instead of the kids.' His face took on a look of sadness. 'It suited her not to have me around. She never consulted me. I love them all equally, but it tears my heart out knowing I've not been there to tuck them in, share all their fears and foibles. And there's been no one to replace me.'

Simon's first wife sometimes shares with Ros, which Ros admits she finds very flattering, and if ever his second wife rings to ask anything about her two children, Simon passes her over to speak to Ros, saying that's her department. There are no visible scars as far as Simon can see. He feels it's as perfect as it can be, that there's harmony all round from Ros to both ex-wives.

'The Lord helped Ros with all the resentment she felt at the beginning with Daphne,' he said. 'The only disharmony is between the first two wives.'

'Yes, that was difficult when they met on the doorstep once, dropping the kids off,' Ros admitted.

With six children and three homes to consider, Ros and Simon have to work a system whereby all the children come together for the whole weekend under one roof—theirs—one weekend in four.

'Sometimes it happens that the middle two are away,' Simon explained, 'but that gives us more time to be on our own with the older two. The more there are the easier it is. They all get on well—enjoy the same sports. We take them out for a meal quite often. Sometimes I take them without Ros so they've just got their Dad.'

'I think that's important,' Ros agreed.

'I only see the good side, of course,' Simon admitted. 'I don't see the bickering.'

Peter and Sandra, more newly married than Simon and Ros, are still in the process of working out the logistics and emotions of two sets of children needing access to their respective absent parents. Sandra's live with her, and when not visiting their own father, are, of course, installed as incumbents of the household when Peter's children visit.

'My kids, at one time, resented enormously that I was with Sandra's children seven days a week and with them only one,' Peter admitted. 'There was this—very natural—resentment when Sandra's three gave me a kiss. I suppose it makes me over-compensate with my three.'

'We have to discipline ourselves in the way we react to them all, and point out to each other the areas we both over-react in,' Sandra agreed.

Peter nodded. 'I felt I had to overcome this enormous hurt I'd inflicted on them.'

'Sometimes we pray with my girls,' Sandra said, 'and point out how Peter's kids feel when they come down. The girls know what it feels like from when they visit their father, who has a step-daughter. They restrain themselves from seeking affection when Peter's kids are down. They hold back.'

Peter affirmed that although they had been able to achieve much with Sandra's girls over a period of time, they have been unable to talk it out with his children. Part of this difficulty has been because of their inability to pray with Peter's children, and his ex-wife's attitudes to Peter's new-found faith.

'She feels I'm a hypocrite when I tell the kids that if they come for the weekend they can come to church with us on Sunday.'

But both he and Sandra feel quite clearly that they have a responsibility in sharing their faith with all the children.

Putting up a name-plate

One further problem can arise in respect of the absent
parent, that of the legalities involved in certain aspects of
the stepfamily. An understanding needs to be reached of
the difference between a care and control order, and
custody. In theory, a parent may have custody without
having care and control, or care and control without
custody, but it is more usual for the custodial parent to
have, if not sole custody, then at least a joint custody.

In simple terms, care and control is to do with the day-
to-day nurturing of the child and the decisions made in
that regard ie feeding, clothing and housing them, hours of
curfew, pocket money and so on. Custody is concerned
with the larger decisions in life: whether the child should
go to boarding school, perhaps even to giving consent in
the case of non-emergency surgery. A parent with the
daily care and control order but no custody must refer all
larger decisions to the custodial parent, even though the
child is not living under that parent's roof. But this type of
order is rare. More usually, the parent with whom the
child resides will have at least a joint say in such matters,
if not sole custody.

Even so, some decisions cannot be made by either
parent alone. For instance, a child may not be taken out of
the country indefinitely without the permission of both
parents, regardless of who has custody or a court order.
Should the stepfather's job necessitate such a move, then
it's perhaps doubtful that any court of law would support
the natural parent in withholding consent.

Neither may the child's religion be changed without the
other parent's consent, though again this would have to be
a pretty drastic change and be against the child's own will
for a court to allow the absent parent to stand against it.

It is as well, also, to check on the legal rights and
responsibilities of the step-parent in the event of the nat-

ural parent's death. A letter from a solicitor-friend seeks to
clarify the matter:

'In theory, the natural parent of the children could seek
their return... It would be sensible for the spouse who was
the natural parent of the children to appoint the step-
parent a testamentary guardian of the child or children, in
his/her will. In that case the guardian would be in a
position to act jointly with the remaining natural parent.
If there was a dispute as to with whom the children were
to live, then it would have to be resolved by the court...'

Under certain circumstances a step-parent may take
out an Adoption Order whereby he/she would take on all
the rights of the natural parent. Without this, however, no
obligation is placed upon the step-parent by the authorities to take responsibility for the children if both natural
parents were to die. Unless other family members step
in—for instance, grandparents—there might be no alternative but for the Council to take them into care.

But it is perhaps in the more common region of name-
changing that most problems occur. Quoting again from
the letter:

'...the consent of the court, or the natural father's
consent would need to be given before a formal change of
name could be made by way of deed poll.... Generally the
court, it seems, will not sanction a change of name unless
it can be clearly shown that it is in the best interests of the
particular child. In practice, however, children often seem
to adopt their stepfather's name...for example in regis-
tration for school. This is in breach of the order normally
made by the court...'

The problem arises in that younger children particularly, often feel insecure in having a different name to
their newly married mother. To be known by a different
surname to other members of the family, especially for the
only child, can be an isolating and divisive experience,

raising embarrassing questions from the child's peer group.

Isobel's children elected to use their stepfather's name when they were in junior school, as she explained.

'Whenever they had to bring letters home they were addressed in my new married name, and the girls wanted to identify. But although they had their father's permission to use Warren's surname, they certainly didn't have their paternal grandmother's.'

Isobel smoothed down her skirt with a little gesture of long-suffering before continuing. 'So although they were known by his name throughout primary and junior school, Gran's wishes were such that she wouldn't pay the school fees unless they were complied with. They are now known by their old name, but they're older and more able to cope with the difference.'

Sandra's children have done likewise, taking on their stepfather's surname, though not by deed poll. I asked whether that had been accomplished smoothly. Peter smiled ruefully.

'Under duress. We had to make their father see that it was very difficult for the girls to have a different name. But when it came to my own children, they didn't want to change their name to their mother's new married name.'

'But my girls did,' Sandra said quite emphatically. 'I think it was Olivia who said, "We shan't have the same name!" '

This difference in attitude could be to do with gender. Peter's eldest is a boy and it may be that boys have stronger feelings about retaining their own surname than girls, who, after all, are used to the fact that women take on a new name in marriage. In this case, however, the two little girls would naturally want to identify with their older brother.

'So having had the issue raised,' Peter continued, 'we sat down and talked about it.' He paused for a moment lost in thought. 'I sometimes wonder if we've done that too much. But we feel they should feel involved and that we listen to them and their ideas, but that the decisions are nevertheless ours. At least that way they feel they have some input.'

With three teenage daughters myself at the time of my second marriage, all of whom chose to keep their own surname without it causing the slightest problem, my only thought for others would be that they should be absolutely sure that what they do really is in the best long-term interests of the children. The Bible tells us that 'the heart is deceitful above all things,'[4] and it is so easy to fool oneself, to rationalise and convince the children in your care that you are motivated purely by love for them, when in reality the subconscious desire to alienate them still further from the absent natural parent may be paramount.

Feelings run high at the time of divorce, but never more so than when one partner re-marries. The one flesh of the first marriage may have been torn asunder, but until the moment of union with another, some sort of bond remains. A second marriage makes you one flesh with another, and severs, as no divorce certificate can ever do, the one flesh of the first marriage. With that in mind, there can be this overwhelming desire to hit back, to cut off the past completely, and to attempt to create a new thing—a family unit without a divisive history.

Children may well believe themselves desirous of a change of name whilst they are young, and this may well be the best way forward. But feelings change. Daughters who declare themselves hypothetically independent of their fathers in their teens, often find, when faced with the reality of their own wedding a few years later, that the ties are not so easily broken. And that deep down, despite previous vociferous assertions to the contrary, they never truly wanted them to be.

Notes

1 2 Corinthians 4:8
2 Malachi 2:16
3 Romans 12:9
4 Jeremiah 17:9

I I

Beyond The Boundaries

Annabel regarded her mother gravely, before lowering her eyes defensively. 'The thing is, Mummy,' she twisted the sparkling new engagement ring on her finger. 'I feel I'd like to...well, I wonder how you would feel...that is, do you think I ought to ask Dad to give me away?'

Penny swallowed hard. For years now, since long before Owen had proposed, Annabel had always been quite vociferous in declaring that nothing would induce her to ask her father to give her away if and when she should be married, nor to invite his wife to her wedding. If she was honest, Penny had found it hard to condemn her elder daughter for her feelings, yet she'd always known, deep down, that when it came to the crunch Annabel would almost certainly soften. And much as she, Penny, disliked the thought of having to socialise with the woman who had been instrumental in breaking up her marriage, she knew she wouldn't be able to live with herself if she let her feelings stand in the way of her daughter's happiness.

'Yes. Definitely,' she replied briskly, seeking to dispel any lingering doubts in Annabel's mind. 'Whatever your father's behaviour in the past, it would be like a slap in the face not to ask him.'

'Well I know I've always said that since he's never really been a father to me, I didn't feel he had the right to give me away, but I suppose he has more right than anyone else.' Annabel flushed, grateful to her mother for not making things difficult.

Talking it all through a few weeks later, with a friend who had had a similar experience the previous year, Penny frankly admitted her feelings.

'Isn't it incredible!' she began. 'You bring them up all these years, making sacrifices, putting up with all their moods, coping with their untidiness and thoughtlessness, yet when the chips are down, their father, who's hardly done a thing for them, can still waltz in and take over. I think children must be like dogs. They get kicked, but still come back and lick your hand. It's not that I want to deny him his rights, or feel envious of the fact that Annabel's asked him to give her away, but...'

'Go on be honest,' Betty laughed uproariously, her round face creasing with good humour, 'it's just plain, good-old-fashioned jealousy. Just like I felt over my son asking his father.'

Penny's worried face relaxed into laughter. 'You're right! I am jealous. If I'm honest, I'd rather he didn't have any part in it at all. But I wouldn't let Anny know that for the world.

'But there are other complications. Already *she's* putting her oar in,' Penny sighed. 'Richard, my "ex", keeps telling me that his wife Angela thinks I should do this and that and the other for the wedding. What's it to do with her I'd like to know? It's not that I still hold anything against her, but I do find it churns me up inside. Annabel's my eldest daughter and I've waited all these years to enjoy arranging her wedding. I don't want some other woman interfering just because she's now married to Anny's father.'

Betty's voice took on a more serious note as she laid a hand on Penny's arm. 'No, of course you don't. And neither should you. It has nothing to do with your "ex's" wife and I think you should make that clear to him.'

Gratefully Penny smiled at her friend. 'It's not even as if Annabel ever lived with them. She's getting rather fed up with it too. When Annabel went to see her father last week, Angela kept telling her that it was no good expecting Richard to wear a grey morning suit because black suited him better. What a cheek to think she could dictate what the bride and groom should have. I can't help feeling that if Anny hadn't asked her father then there wouldn't be all these complications.'

'I felt just the same,' Betty confessed quietly. 'When my son asked his Dad, I thought, "What's he ever done for him?" He walked out whilst Pete was only a toddler. Then I discovered that Pete had been seeing him on and off for some time without ever letting on to me. It was like a knife in my back.'

'That's it. You can get divorced, but you're never really free from all the emotional entanglements when you have children. Blood's thicker than water, and whatever he's done, he's the only father they have. There are always bonds, even if it's a love-hate relationship.'

When Penny shared this conversation with Maurice later in the day, he endorsed Betty's view that Richard should be told that Angela was not to interfere in the arrangements. 'As far as I'm concerned it's between the bride's parents and the groom's parents. If you think it'll help, you can tell Richard that I shall take a back seat too,' Maurice offered.

'But I welcome your advice,' Penny protested.

'Yes, well you'll have it,' Maurice smiled. 'Anything I can do I will. But I should just keep quiet about it.'

The situation was rather different, Penny reflected, in that Annabel had lived under Maurice's roof for some years, whereas she'd had little real contact with her father and his wife. Annabel obviously felt likewise.

'I do feel that Maurice should have some place of honour in all the proceedings,' she told her mother. 'We feel we'd like him to read the lesson during the service and play a fairly prominent part.'

During their enforced contact, Richard offered Penny a financial contribution towards the wedding. Though she would have preferred not to have had that link but to have borne the cost alone, she realised that it would not only be unfair to Maurice to saddle him with the financial burden of his step-daughter's nuptials, but also churlish to refuse Richard's offer. Reluctantly she accepted, and between them they agreed a global figure.

With the situation made clear regarding the exclusion (at least ostensibly) of the step-parents in the decision-making, Richard gave Penny a free hand, and though this meant she had the brunt of the donkey-work, she appreciated the liberty of not having to go cap-in-hand for every penny, nor to refer every quotation or cost direct to him. Scrupulously, Penny kept account of every expense so that, if Richard should so wish, he could see clearly where the money had gone.

Even so, as the day drew closer, Penny remarked to her mother, 'It seems to me that the bride's mother does all the hard work for a wedding, and yet the father waltzes in on the day and has all the limelight.'

Battling in the basement

Time and again, as a Christian, Penny found herself at the foot of the cross. 'I'm sorry Lord,' she wept, 'I'm as jealous as can be. I thought I'd got over all this, but I'm just as bad as ever. I know it sounds pathetic and self-pitying Lord, but when I think of all the years I've spent bringing the girls up alone before you brought Maurice into my life, I just can't bear the way their father gets away with waltzing in and out of their lives whenever it suits him.

'I'm ashamed to admit it Lord, but the dark side of me wishes they'd just tell him where to get off. I hate myself for feeling like that, but that's the truth. It's only because I know your love Lord, and the way you've forgiven me down through the years, that I have it in me at all to hold out the olive branch to Richard. That and the fact that I know it would be damaging to the girls themselves if I were to encourage anything less than love in them for their father.

'It's been hard Lord, putting his side to them whenever they have turned against him, always encouraging them to see things from his perspective as a non-Christian. Without you Lord, I'd never have had it in me to help them to see that we have to forgive him just as you forgave us— whilst we were still sinners.

'Have you allowed me to go through all this now Lord—all the jealousy and heart-searching—just to remind me that it's only by grace I'm saved? That "old-man" is still there in me, isn't he Lord? There's never going to be a time when the heat is off and the battle won—at least not this side of the grave. Your Word says, "If we claim to be without sin we deceive ourselves and the truth is not in us." But if we confess our sin Lord, you are faithful and just and will forgive us and purify us from all unrighteousness.[1]

'Lord, I'm sorry I'm here yet again confessing my sin and asking your forgiveness. It's only because you forgive "seventy times seven"[2] that I dare to keep coming—that and the fact that you've already died for these sins, and tomorrow's and next week's. It would just be a waste of your death if I didn't avail myself of your pardon. By your Spirit, Lord, cleanse me and purify me and give me the grace and the love to go through with this wedding as

Jesus would. Make me more Christlike Lord, for your glory's sake...'

Spring-cleaning the cellar

A wedding, perhaps more than any other celebration, has the potential for bringing out the worst in divorced parents, rekindling the warring factions, opening up the battle-scars and rubbing salt into the wounds. And yet, as Penny discovered, it has the potential too for growth, for identifying those areas still not wholly under the sway of the Holy Spirit, where the enemy is still able to make himself felt.

In committing himself to complete the good work begun in us to transform us into the likeness of Jesus, it is necessary for God to help us see ourselves as we really are. With the spotlight turned on those dark corners of the cellar, we can then begin, with the help of the Holy Spirit, the task of spring-cleaning as he blows like a mighty wind to rid our lives of the cobwebs of self-deceit and untruth. Only as we submit to him, relying on his strength in our battle to clear out the accumulated debris of years past, can we hope for order to be restored.

And just as we would use a disinfectant to combat dirt-borne germs, so too we need the powerful action of his cleansing and purifying to purge us of our unrighteousness.

One mother, having thus submitted herself, found that with all her hardness swept away, God was enabled to work in a new way on her ex-husband.

'He was being thoroughly unpleasant about our daughter's wedding plans,' she recalled, 'and whereas I might once have retaliated, I was so mindful of my own sin, I just broke down and cried as he went on and on at me on the telephone. Amazingly, it completely disarmed him. He ended up apologising for his unpleasantness and agreeing with all I'd arranged. I know that wouldn't have happened if I'd given him as good as he was giving me.'

As far as Annabel's wedding was concerned, all passed off happily enough with Richard accompanying his daughter up the aisle, but though he stood at her side throughout the service, the words 'Who giveth this woman to be married to this man?' were omitted, as Annabel felt this would be a hypocrisy. Likewise, when it came to the speeches, she asked a long-standing family friend to speak on her behalf, feeling that her father could have little to say in that respect. And to give him his due, he was more than happy with the arrangement.

Although a buffet meal might have been easier in many respects, the bride and groom elected to have a wedding breakfast. They felt this would be less demanding in terms of introductions and conversations with relatives from the severed family, which might have proved strained. This was followed by an evening disco, open to all those precluded by cost from the formal affair. After considerable dispute amongst all parties, seating at the top table was eventually resolved with the bride's father accompanying the groom's mother, and with her consent, since she was a widow, Maurice accompanied Penny who would otherwise have been alone. Angela, Richard's second wife, sat with friends at one of the side tables.

These sorts of problems are peculiar to the stepfamily and have to be faced with equanimity. At the point of divorce and remarriage, such difficulties and the emotional trauma they raise may be completely unthought of, or at very least envisaged so far in the future that they hold no spectre until imminent. Coming of age, whether celebrated at eighteen or twenty-one, weddings, the arrival of grandchildren, Christenings and baptisms are part of the fabric of family life, the traditions and rituals designed to hold families together. For the stepfamily they can be a nightmare, a minefield so fraught with danger it may threaten to blast the family apart still further.

Triumphal arch, or doorway of difficulty?

Yet one of the traditions which comes annually is Christmas, and this can be a preparation for those future, more distant events. Carrying as many of the emotional ties as the more personal celebrations of birthdays and nuptials, the festival commemorating the birth of our Lord Jesus Christ, itself a period of peace and goodwill, can be a time for honest soul searching in how we perpetrate the coming of that Kingdom in our own lives.

In the midst of the turmoil and stress, can we know the reality of the Peace of Jesus and display it to others? The Bible is nothing if not realistic, recognising that this may not always be feasible, but that we can only do our best: 'If it is possible, as far as it depends on you, live at peace with everyone.'[3] We can't be held responsible for the actions of others, but we still have to live through the consequences.

Sandra, mother of three girls, admitted how difficult that can be. 'Last year their father wanted the girls to go to him for Christmas, and they didn't want to go. I suggested we have them for lunch and he for the evening, but he didn't want that because he and his second wife wanted to go to the pub, so they decided to celebrate Christmas Day a day early.'

However, despite the seemingly mutual agreement to this arrangement, Sandra's ex-husband turned it back on her the following year, implying that she had prevented the girls from going to him last year, and that it was, therefore, now his turn to have them.

Peter, Sandra's second husband, pointed out the complications this would cause when it came to attending church. 'We have a similar problem with my children and trying to tie the two families together,' he admitted.

'When I raise the question, my ex-wife says, "Oh it's too far in advance." Then when it's nearer the time, she makes the decision alone. She won't let us have them at all on Christmas Day. Before Sandra and I married, I used to go up at 3 pm and have two hours in her front room while she was at the back of the house. But it was stifling.'

Peter shifted his position. 'She had everything when we split up, I took nothing. But going back into the house I was made to feel this small.' He indicated between finger and thumb.

For Warren and Isobel the problems over where the children should spend their Christmases are perhaps only just beginning to loom on the horizon.

'The girls are beginning to feel it's only fair to spend time with their father,' Isobel admitted honestly. 'And that causes problems for me because I don't want it.'

Fencing off the future

When it came to the question of a coming-of-age party, she was even more unsure.

'I shy away from it because I can't face it,' she cried with a shudder. 'I think they'll have to have two parties. And they know it—they know it wouldn't work between us. I think my "ex" would expect to take over and for us to fit in.'

Warren nodded slowly, his brow puckered as he thought through the issues. 'I must be honest, I couldn't have a party in our house with their father. It would have to be somewhere else. And I still wouldn't be happy with it.'

'It bothers me a lot, especially a wedding,' Isobel confessed. 'I see our family as a unit. I feel it would be destroyed by my "ex" and his wife coming as a couple.'

'What about their father giving the girls away?' I asked, turning to Warren.

'I'd accept that,' he said slowly. 'I wouldn't like it, but there's not much I could do about it...'

'I would resent it on Warren's behalf because he's brought them up,' Isobel interrupted stingingly.

Warren shrugged and pursed his lips. 'I think Tracy will just turn up married one day...'

With her own two daughters living away from home, and a widow herself, Doreen put her heart and soul into giving Jeff's daughter the sort of eighteenth birthday party *she* wanted.

'It wasn't what Jeff and I would have chosen,' she admitted. 'But I felt Natasha should have it her way. It cost quite a lot of money, hiring a hall and having a disco and DJ, even though I did all the catering.'

News filtered back to Doreen that Natasha's mother had been making cruel remarks amongst the family, about her's and Jeff's 'meanness' in not having outside caterers in. But rising above the hurt, Doreen was able to put it behind her.

'I've met her,' Doreen told me, 'and felt I must be civil and talk to her for Natasha's sake, but I must admit, I wasn't really looking forward to the party.'

Still, Doreen's positive attitudes paid off, and she was thrilled with a remark made by her step-daughter shortly before the big day. She smiled as she recalled. 'When I wouldn't let Natasha open her presents early, I told her I was treating her the same as my own daughters. And she said, "Well, I am your daughter now, aren't I?" '

Grandparents—the golden gateway

It's perhaps hard to remember at times that in-laws, the butt of musical hall jokes for years, can also be grand-parents, beloved of their grandchildren, and a golden gateway to freedom for harassed mums. In his wisdom,

God ordained that each family unit should have two sets of grandparents; for the stepfamily, life is not so simple!

Step-parents and step-children have a hard row to hoe. Most people find it difficult enough having to contend with one set of in-laws. To those embarking upon a second marriage, everything doubles up (or trebles, or even quadruples), and this is more so for the children, who from only one remarriage on each side may well now have as many as six sets of 'grandparents' to whom to relate, some of whom will have no blood tie:

Parents of their parents	= 2 pairs grandparents
Parents of father's new wife	= 1 pair 'grandparents'
In-laws of father's new wife (if previously married)	= 1 pair 'grandparents'
Parents of mother's new husband	= 1 pair grandparents
In-laws of mother's new husband (if previously married)	= 1 pair grandparents

All will, most probably, be intent upon maintaining a relationship with their grandchildren and may well feel that the new partner poses a threat in this respect. Indeed, these feelings may well be justified. Where re-marriage necessitates a move from one part of the country to another, contact may well be severed, either intentionally—in a desire to cut loose from a painful past and make a fresh start—or simply through neglect.

One elderly couple were devastated when, within a year or two of losing their son through a tragic illness, they then 'lost' their grandchildren too when their daughter-in-law remarried and moved far away. Without an ongoing relationship, the probability of the children ever visiting their grandparents alone seems remote. And it's doubtful that the older couple themselves would ever feel comfortable about visiting the home of their daughter-in-law's new husband, even if they were to be invited.

But as well as the untold anguish felt by the grand-parents themselves in a situation like this, there are others who inflict further pain upon the new partnership, per-haps through jealousy of a new daughter-in-law or son-in-law. And when the stepmother is called to mediate between grandmother and grandchild, this could further strain the in-law relationship.

'When we had the children on Boxing Day one year, we had Philip's Mum too,' Gina recalled. 'She's not easy, but the girls like to see her. There was an argument that went on and on between her and one of Philip's children, and Grandma eventually asked to be taken home.'

'I felt my Mum was being totally unreasonable,' Philip commented.

Gina had to take his daughter on one side and explain that Grandma was just cross because she'd argued back with her, and that if Gilly would just say she was sorry for answering back, all would be well.

'So she came down,' Gina explained, 'sobbing her heart out and said "I'm sorry Grandma." '

Philip snorted. 'All my mother said was: "I should think so too." '

Sometimes the problem of possessiveness in grand-parents can cause problems even before a second marriage takes place. And this will almost certainly be exacerbated if there are other children involved.

'We had major problems with my mother,' Margot told us regretfully. 'She felt her grandchildren had their nose pushed out by Barrie's children. I think she hates them.' Margot shook her head disbelievingly. 'She had planned that I could go out to work after my divorce, so that *she* could have my kids. So she hates Barrie even more, because by marrying me he prevented that happening.'

'Yes,' Barrie nodded. 'But the other complication was that Margot's mother-in-law, who was very close to Mar-got during her first marriage, doesn't get on with my ex-wife.' Since Barrie's ex-wife had married Margot's ex-husband, she had become the new daughter-in-law.

'She felt she had to come down secretly to see her grandchildren,' Margot continued. 'The whole relationship between herself and Jayne has just deteriorated....'

Sadly, there seems little in the way of action that one can take to alleviate a situation like this. But however tempting it may be to pat oneself on the back and feel secretly vindicated if your ex-in-laws have a better relationship with you than with the new husband or wife, just remember the situation could be reversed, as it was, to start with, for Simon and Ros.

'Simon used to take me over to his mother's,' Ros told us, 'but it took a long time before we got on.'

'She thought a lot of my first wife,' Simon explained. 'They still see a lot of each other. I don't think that deep down my mother has ever really forgiven me for leaving her.'

Jeff and Doreen, forewarned by another family member as soon as they returned from honeymoon of possible friction between Jeff's mother and her new daughter-in-law, were able, tactfully, to avert any conflict.

'My parents had happily accepted Jeff's children as part of the family,' Doreen told us, 'so that was no problem. But Jeff's mother, who had kept telling us before we got married how glad she was that she would no longer have to come over daily to cook and clean for him and his children, actually didn't want to let go when it came to it.' She paused for a moment, then went on, 'I felt really bad about pushing her out, but I knew it wouldn't work if she kept coming over.'

Jeff took up the story. 'We had to be very tactful,' he recalled. 'My brother told me she was expecting to come over as usual, so the first night back from honeymoon, I went to see her and asked her over for dinner on the

Wednesday—several days later. That way, she knew she wasn't expected before that.'

Jeff's mother took the hint, and though Doreen felt awkward for some time, the two women have subsequently hit it off reasonably well.

But the clash isn't always between daughter-in-law and mother-in-law, as Isobel recounted. Although her mother-in-law had a good deal to say to her grandchildren against their father after he left home, once Warren came on the scene she made up with her own son.

'She was obviously afraid of not seeing the girls any more,' Isobel admitted. 'But she began saying to the girls that Warren wasn't their father and that he shouldn't be in their house.'

Solicitors' letters were sent making unreasonable demands for access, and the whole situation threatened to get out of hand until the court sent a social worker around to review the circumstances. On the strength of her assessment, the terms of access then agreed were in fact less favourable to father and grandmother than they had originally been.

Whilst with their father, the children often come into contact with his second wife's parents. 'They refer to them by their Christian names,' Isobel explained. 'I know they go to see them sometimes and have presents from them, but they never show them to me.'

Peter's mother is a widow. She makes a definite distinction between her natural grandchildren and the others, he and Sandra told me, giving pocket money to the former but excluding Sandra's three. This attitude hurt Sandra considerably and threatened to cause upsets between the children. Eventually it was agreed that she should give the money quietly so that Sandra's children would not know. Although such divisive and secret action may seem unfair to some, it may be that Peter's mother feels that Sandra's children have their own grandparents to provide such treats.

This particular aspect of the stepfamily—step-grandparents—is a grey area. My own in-laws are kindness itself, and without grandchildren of their own have been very generous with gifts to the girls. But with the best will in the world, there never can be the same rapport which exists between most natural grandparents and their children's offspring. The older the grandchildren, the less likely is it that a close relationship will grow between them and their stepgrandparents, though Doreen's family seem to have accomplished this against all odds.

'How about the children from both sides?' I asked, recalling that Doreen's eldest was married and her younger daughter had moved into a flat near her maternal grandparents in her own hometown.

'Well,' Doreen smiled happily, 'Jeff's daughter Natasha had her eighteenth birthday a few days ago, and my Amy couldn't find an 18th card with 'Sister' on, so she wrote it on. I think Natasha felt quite overwhelmed, and all my family—my sisters and aunts, as well as my parents, swamped her with presents. But then, we've always been a demonstrative family.'

Perhaps this is the key. Some families will naturally find it easier to embrace new members into the fold, whilst with others good family relationships may take time to develop, and even then may never exactly match your expectations. We can't all be cast in the same mould. How dull life would be if we were!

Extensions to the family home

Additions to the family may be seen by different members as either a further complication to an already difficult situation, or as a particular blessing which unifies and draws together each individual in a unique and wonderful way.

There is good reason for a unifying bond to be felt between all family members, because the new baby provides a genetic link between the mother and all her other offspring, and the father and all his other children. This link may of itself go some way toward cementing together the tenuous relationships of the stepfamily. Enlarged upon by sensitive parents emphasising the bond, it may actually prove the catalyst through which a deep and enduring love grows amongst members of the stepfamily.

But many parents may doubt the wisdom of adding yet another human life, with its own particular characteristics, to the already intricate mélange of interwoven personalities. If ever you have seen a lace maker at work you will know what I mean. With nimble fingers and complex movements, the cotton bobbins are shuttled around pins on a cushion to form something breathtakingly beautiful. But be it Honiton lace or Nottingham lace, precise patterns have to be followed, and the introduction of yet another bobbin or a further pair of pins would completely ruin the finished article.

This must have been the fear of Vincent and his first wife when his first child (her second) was born. His wife's daughter Jocelyn, whom he adopted, was only three years of age at the time. So disturbed was she by the advent of another baby, that she played up all night, every night— even before her half brother was born. But being so young, this may have been no more than the normal reaction of any first child in a family even where no second marriage has taken place.

Be that as it may it is very evident from Jocelyn's life today that all is not as it should be. An unmarried teenage mother twice over, both with different men, there is at least a suggestion that her own childhood security may have been lacking, and that her essays into the world of sex and romance were an ill-founded attempt to find love.

Vincent admits quite freely too that his own mother, Jocelyn's adoptive stepgrandmother, has never accepted her and refuses even to acknowledge that she is now a great-grandmother.

For other families the question is hypothetical.

'We have conflicting views on this,' Isobel said frankly, 'but I'm glad that I can't have babies since my hysterectomy, though that's unfair on Warren. But he knew that before he married me.'

'Obviously that was the hardest decision,' Warren admitted honestly, 'because I wanted children. And as I have only two sisters, the family name will die with me.'

Isobel's girls openly admit to feeling more secure because they're the only ones on the scene at home. Their father's wife hadn't been married before so to date there are no other children involved. But the girls feel very threatened by the thought that he could father another baby, and have told their mother that the subject has come up a couple of times when they've been visiting him.

'We actually had to ring and ask so we could know how to handle it because they were in such a state,' Isobel told me, adding that their paternal grandmother had told them not to be so selfish.

Two families who have succeeded admirably in integrating step-children with their half brothers and sisters are Leslie and Laura and Ros and Simon. Since Leslie's girls were in their teens, with all their maternal instincts coming to the fore when Laura's two little ones were born, there was no sense of competition. Neither, as the two older girls lived with their mother, was there any question of deprivation in pecking order. Rather, the two babies were a constant source of delight to all involved, and probably, if truth be told, ensured the girls' visiting their father rather more often than might otherwise have been the case!

For Ros and Simon, however, the situation was more complex. Though Patsy was quite little when Ros was expecting her first child, she was delighted with the prospect of a new baby.

'I bought a book and showed her what was happening during my pregnancy,' Ros told me. 'She was only four, but we really shared through the pictures. She really could understand.'

Simon smiled. 'Kevin took it all in his stride... "So what...no big deal...what's for tea".'

'But it was a good opportunity to teach him the facts of life,' Ros said emphatically. 'He was interested. He'd get the book down.'

With the new babies four and five years of age, I wondered how the older children react now.

Patsy does feel a bit put out now because she's no longer the baby of the family,' Ros admitted, adding that sometimes when Patsy has been to see her mother, where she is still treated as the baby, she may react adversely for a while when she returns to being the older sister.

'But she's back to normal the next day,' Ros laughed.

'And Kevin's a good boy, very good,' his father said fondly. 'He helps us with bringing up the two little ones. He lets us sleep in and he's even changed the baby's nappy.'

When asked how fatherhood had affected him, Simon admitted he had felt too old to be bothered with nappies again. 'But it was the broken nights I found difficult,' he said good humouredly. 'I think I'm a better father now than when I was younger.

'It's just the pressures of business, and leading a house-group, plus a young family.... It can be very demanding. With six kids to support and babies waking you up at nights.... I see colleagues with small mortgages, teenage children, all settled, playing golf; sometimes I feel under a lot of pressure. But I wouldn't swap with any of those people that I envy when I'm tired. I love those little ones. I appreciate what I've got so much more. I really enjoy pottering around with them.'

So, what are the lessons to be learned when it comes to relating to ex-spouses, grandparents and new babies? Perhaps they are quite simply that there are few practical solutions, only the outworking of love-and-forgiveness— the agape love of which Paul's letter to the Corinthians speaks so eloquently: the patience, kindness, unenvious meekness and humility; the gentleness, selflessness, forgiving and forgetting, protecting, trusting, hoping and persevering.[4] With these qualities alone can the acts of sinful nature be overcome, the hatred, discord, jealousy, rage, selfish ambition, dissensions, factions and envy which the Bible tells us are a bar to inheriting the Kingdom of God.[5]

Throughout the Old Testament every story of stepfamilies depicts the problems, the jealousies, the insecurities, from Hagar's son Ishmael, of whom it is recorded that his descendents 'lived in hostility towards all their brothers',[6] through the hatred of Joseph by his stepbrothers[7] to the enmity and murder between Absalom and Amnon, David's sons by different wives[8].

In some ways it makes depressing reading. Yet God used every one of those situations to bring about his purposes. As we shall see in that most beautiful story of a stepfamily, Ruth and her mother-in-law Naomi. And in the life of Jesus, we see the ultimate in stepfamily relationships.

Notes

[1] 1 John 1:8
[2] Matthew 18:22
[3] Romans 12:18
[4] 1 Corinthians 13

[5] Galatians 5:19, 20
[6] Genesis 25:18
[7] Genesis 37:4
[8] 2 Samuel 13

12

Windows On The World

The young woman who sat before Penny was attractive, well-groomed and articulate. Someone who, at first sight, would seem to have no reason for problems in her life. Yet as Penny poured the tea and passed her visitor a cup, she watched as Nova's face began to crumple. Moving swiftly, Penny sat beside her guest, and taking the cold hand in her own, waited until the tears were spent.

Nova's story was little different to others she'd heard of broken marriages, divorce, remarriage and then a long slow painful discovery of being 'outside God's will'. It was heartbreaking to learn of Christians who, desperately hurt by a first partner and the disintegration of their marriage, in their vulnerability had temporarily taken their eyes off the Lord. And in their desire to love and be loved, they had not always stopped to consider whether this second marriage really did have God's blessing. How easy it is, where affairs of the heart are concerned, to rationalise, to believe that the desire of my heart is also the desire of the Lord's heart for me.

'I feel as if God is punishing me,' Nova wept. 'Everything's going wrong between Terry and me, and I just feel so guilty all the time.'

During the course of the next hour or so, Penny was able to ascertain the circumstances of the situation, the

reasons for the divorce, and the spiritual state of both
Terry and Nova at the time of their second marriage.
Gently she attempted to lead Nova to see that though she
had almost certainly stepped outside God's will, in that
her divorce from her first husband did not comply with the
Scriptural grounds for divorce, she did not have to stay
there.

Our God is a God of new beginnings. His Word tells us
that there is 'no condemnation for those who are in Christ
Jesus'[1]. So when the Holy Spirit of God convicts us of sin,
it is only that he may bring us back into the fold. 'If we
confess our sins, he is faithful and just and will forgive us
our sins and purify us from all unrighteousness.'[2]

What wonderful news! To know that we need never be
outside God's perfect will for our lives. For once back
inside the fold, we have the same Shepherd and are under
the same protection as the rest of the flock, we are guided
in the same paths and graze in the same pastures. There is
no second-best for a child of God. We may make mistakes,
we may wander from the pathway, wilfully or through the
distractions of this world which take our eyes off the
Shepherd. But he will leave the flock, to go in search of the
one lost sheep. And when he finds it, far from condemning, 'he joyfully puts it on his shoulders and goes home.'[3],
telling his neighbours that this is a time of rejoicing. For
'there is more rejoicing in heaven over one sinner who
repents than over ninety-nine righteous persons who do
not need to repent.'[4]

Obscure glass

The arguments over divorce and remarriage have been
debated down through the centuries, and continue to gen-
erate as much confusion and misunderstanding as
illumination upon the matter. Whatever one's personal
views, there is no getting away from the fact that the

church, as much as the world, is now having to face the reality of divorced and remarried folk in their midst. Gone are the days when Christians could sit back self-righteously and feel that this was a problem of the world which, however pitiable, did not impinge upon the respectability of the church.

God said quite clearly in Malachi 2:16: 'I hate divorce.' But nowhere does he condemn the divorcee, or charge us to do likewise. On the contrary, of the woman caught in adultery, Jesus said, 'If any one of you is without sin, let him be the first to throw a stone at her.'[5] The fact is that marriage itself is under attack—yours and mine—every bit as much as the family down the road with an unemployed father and four children of primary school age. In fact Christian marriage is more under attack than most, since Satanists pray regularly for its demise.

Of course divorce is not part of God's ideal will. But neither is famine in the Third World. Nor AIDS. Nor drug addiction. Yet can any of us honestly say that we are innocent of the growth of these evils in society? We *are* the society who has allowed these evils. We cannot exonerate ourselves. All intercessory prayer in the Bible is based on an acknowledgement of national and corporate culpability.

Nor, when it comes to the guilt felt by people like Nova, are we innocent in our attitudes. We may long to reach out, to help those who are hurting. Yet in our hearts, mingled with that compassion, and perhaps because we are unsure of the facts and can't face up to the turmoil of confusion, how often do we metaphorically turn away and cross the road to avoid facing the issue?

Unable to sort out our own minds on the issues of divorce and remarriage, have we simply taken the easy way out by pretending the problem doesn't exist? If so, we, the church, have become the modern day priest and Levite, with stepfamilies and the like lying beaten and

neglected by the side of the road, and secular organisations like Gingerbread and Stepfamily attempting to be
the Good Samaritan.

Sometimes, if we're honest, the pity we feel for such
people is at least in part a feeling that there must be some
inadequacy in their make-up, something lacking in their
relationships, and that many of their problems are self-
inflicted. Deep down, there may be a smugness in our own
respectable, till-death-us-do-part marriages.

It may be no more than a subconscious attitude. Yet I
know, if I'm honest, that I felt like this about others before
my own divorce. And I suspect that even where the death
of a partner has brought about a stepfamily situation,
some of these thoughts can prevail.

It's hard to be this honest with ourselves. But if this is
so, we need the cleansing power of the Holy Spirit to purge
us of judgemental attitudes and to pour into our hearts the
unconditional love of God for others.

Warren, when asked how he felt marrying a divorcee,
admitted to deep feelings when it came to facing both the
world and the church.

'To begin with it was difficult. Your own insecurity can
make you feel a second-class citizen, but if you're confident....' He paused, before continuing brightly, 'I've never
really cared what other people think. I know as a Christian I perhaps shouldn't say that, but if we, as a family,
are happy then it's up to other people to sort out their
problem if they feel we're inferior in some way.'

Isobel agreed. 'I certainly feel that as a stepfamily or as
a single parent family the children are viewed differently
in school. All behavioural problems tend to go on being
pinned on them throughout school life, although they may
have been resolved.'

It would seem, despite the world's maxim that since
divorce and remarriage are now so commonplace people
take it in their stride, that the feelings are still there.

Brazened out, with an attitude of 'that's their problem', or pushed under in denial, the stepfamily is still dogged with a sense of being found inadequate in some way. And this is true too in the church.

'I felt second-class for a good twelve months with the church,' Warren confessed. 'But we felt we were so strong as a family right from the start, so we never felt any real pressure from outside.'

Again Isobel agreed. 'The people in the church who know us accept us for what we are, but those who don't know us tend not to. We're fairly unique in our fellowship.'

'I find people assume we're a natural family and refer to the girls as my daughters,' Paul said, aware of a personal dilemma. 'I find it embarrassing, almost deceptive, not to correct them, though once they know we're a stepfamily I don't mind. Do you find you can't avoid telling new folk you're a stepfamily?'

'No, not really,' Isobel replied. 'It's more in the Bible study it may come up. Sometimes I share some of the things the Lord has shown me through my second marriage.' She paused, pushing back her hair as she thought through the issues. 'I must admit I sometimes feel uncomfortable with some of the Scripture. Not because I feel in the wrong, I know I'm all right. But because I feel others may be condemning me.'

Much of what Warren and Isobel shared was also the experience of Peter and Sandra, particularly when it came to the children coping at school.

'There has been a certain amount of pressure on the children,' Peter admitted, 'but whether it's self-imposed or from other people, I don't know.'

'They find it difficult to answer questions from the other children like, "Which dad do you like best?"' Sandra added. 'Obviously they feel a loyalty to their natural father.'

Peter raised his eyebrows. 'Then they had to do a family tree, and they didn't know how to put me into the family...'

'The youngest one substituted Peter for her father,' Sandra said with concerned amusement, 'then she put all her stepbrothers and sisters in as if they were real. But the eldest put an extra branch on because she wanted to include them all. It got very complicated and the paper wasn't big enough.'

As a teacher, Paul often overhears curious enquiries from children who view the stepfamily with fascination, as something of a phenomenon. Questions like the 'Which dad do you like best?' are commonplace. But it's when children admit to having several 'dads' or 'mums' that your heart goes out to them, as you wonder what sort of people they will grow into from the confused mess of their childhood, and what sort of parents they will make themselves?

When it came to acceptance from the church, Sandra admitted she wasn't sure. 'I don't know how much is me feeling this, but there are people at church who won't sit next to me.'

'Someone actually sat next to you, then got up and moved away for no apparent reason didn't they?' Peter said, confirming that this was not simply Sandra's imagination.

Sandra nodded. 'I know those who've said, "Fancy the church remarrying Sandra." ' She looked to Peter for confirmation.

'People have jumped to conclusions without knowing the details, and without considering that we've had to satisfy the pastors,' he agreed.

Sandra smiled sadly. 'You have to remember that the church has known me as part of a family unit with someone else. Sometimes I wish I could explain, but you can't. It's not their business.'

Peter sat in silence for a moment. 'If I were to sum up my feelings about how both the world and church have reacted to us as step-parents, there isn't a lot of difference,' he said quietly. 'People are people and tend to judge on human standards. If they have a background of personal experience, that tends to colour their judgement.'

Paul looked surprised. 'I thought the world might be more tolerant because Christians aren't so used to the idea,' he remarked.

'They like to think they have higher standards,' Peter agreed, 'but they're all still people. People in the world judge you for what you are now, not what's in the past.'

Sandra shrugged. 'God's blessed us in a family unit and we're part of the greater family, so we've got to give and forgive,' she said. 'You can't expect people to reach out to you. You've got to be prepared to reach out to them.'

'Mmm,' Peter nodded. 'We're all members of the human race. But the second link is that we have Jesus, and you have to build on that.'

Simon's experience was quite different. A member of a housechurch when he was newly converted, he was prayerfully advised by the elders that the intimacy of his relationship with Ros outside wedlock was not right in the eyes of God. But for the sake of the children, who had already lost one mother, it was felt that Ros should not be asked to leave the family home where she'd lived with Simon and the two little ones for about two years. When asked how he felt the body of the church had viewed his situation, his reply was surprising.

'It was the total acceptance that got to me,' he said quietly. 'No one got at us. They didn't know whether we were making love or not.' He paused for a moment, still obviously moved by the quality of love he'd found in the church.

'If the Lord accepts me "as I am",' he went on, 'then I certainly think other Christians should. We've had no problem. Sometimes I suppose it's guilt on the part of the person which makes them feel they are being judged.'

It is significant of the extent of the church's acceptance that Simon has been in a position of leadership for some years. This has ranged from housegroup leader to helping in the leading of Sunday worship, teaching, and giving of communion. And for those who would condemn, it's as well to remember that Moses and David, two of the greatest men of God in the Bible's reckoning, were guilty of murder and adultery.

Dirty window panes

Isn't this really the point? That when it comes down to it, God is more merciful than man? Over the centuries, the church has gone away from the simplicity of Jesus' total forgiveness and has created hoops to be jumped through and barriers to debar those whose lives seem, on the surface, to be less than perfect. One can't help feeling that with so much confusion reigning amongst the church hierarchy, it's no wonder that people like Nova face guilt and insecurity in their second marriages. Without proper teaching and support from the church, these are the pressures most likely to cause the second marriage to fail.

'Remarriage, like adultery, seems to be the unforgivable sin as far as the church at large is concerned,' Paul said one evening as we sat with Warren and Isobel.

'The Church of England certainly sees you as second-class,' Isobel nodded emphatically. 'You don't quite get the same treatment as first-marrieds.'

Strongly defensive of others in her situation, Isobel recalled an event in her home church. 'The Archdeacon spoke on divorce recently,' she said, 'condemning and isolating those who were. I tackled him about it because anyone who was insecure would have felt really rejected. That's the attitude that prevails. You can get past it with individuals, but the church itself is split. Anything that happens in your family, people blame on your status.'

In the 'free' church, similar attitudes tend to prevail. Though outwardly condoning remarriage, at least of the 'innocent partner' (after careful screening and counselling), many churches nevertheless distinguish between those who are married for the first time and those who are in second marriages. Some Baptist Churches refuse to let those who have remarried hold office, though ironically, their spouse may do so! It seems that although remarriage is seen as a 'bad witness' on the part of the partner married for the second time, their partner is not seen to be implicated in any way!

Basing this ruling on the Timothy verse on Deacons, the implication is that anyone married for the second time cannot be the 'husband of but one wife'[6] (or vice versa). As a remarried woman myself I find this not only hurtful, but indicative of a complete misunderstanding of the Scripture. For if I am the wife of two husbands, then I must be an adulteress. And if that is the case, the church had no business remarrying me.

Moreover, if remarriage is to be a bar against holding office, shouldn't being the parents of wayward children also be a disqualification from leadership? The implications are frightening. How many ministers, deacons, lay readers, PCC members, even Bishops and Archdeacons would be left holding the fort if the letter of the law were complied with?

Letting in the sunlight

Could it be, I wonder, that in the case of being the 'husband of but one wife', Paul is addressing, not those who have been remarried (in which case widows and widowers would also be barred), but those who indulged in polygamy, either openly through multiple marriages, or secretly through adulterous relationships? Bearing in mind that sexual involvement with another is seen in the Bible as being 'one flesh', and the notoriously debauched society from which many were being converted to Christianity at the time of writing his epistle, this would at least seem a possibility.

Though few Christians these days would hold divorce against any born-again believer, many may feel that the church has no business remarrying divorcees. Guy Duty, in his book *Divorce and Remarriage*,[7] points out that this is a misunderstanding of the Scriptures: that under Deuteronomic law divorce dissolved a marriage in such a way as to allow the woman to 'go and be another man's wife.' Quoting from Deuteronomy 24:3, 4, Guy Duty goes on to say, 'When the woman married the second time, she did not have two husbands because God spoke of the first as her *former* husband.'

He further goes on to point out that in answering the question on divorce in Matthew 5:32, Jesus shows that it was assumed that remarriage would follow divorce. In pointing out that there were certain situations where divorce would not be acceptable, Jesus' words imply that the reverse is true in other cases.

In other words, if a man divorces his wife unjustly, he is guilty of exposing her to the sin she commits with another man should she enter into a sexual relationship with him (whether by marriage or not). But where a sexual relationship outside the marriage has already broken the 'one flesh' relationship within the marriage, then divorce leaves the couple free to remarry.

Guy Duty stresses that remarriage after divorce was not the issue. The case rests on whether the divorce is permissible or not. And if it is, then remarriage is automatically an equally permissible option. If divorce is not permissible, then it is only separation and remarriage cannot occur.

A further cause for allowable divorce (and therefore remarriage) is found in 1 Corinthians 7:10–15. Here, as Guy Duty shows, if the unbeliever departs, the Christian is told to 'let him depart. A brother or sister is not under bondage in such cases.'

One further reason for divorce (and therefore remarriage) is expounded by Roger Price. He points out that for the person divorced prior to conversion, remarriage is an allowable option, in that conversion makes us a 'new creation, the old has passed away'.[8] *

A thorough study and understanding, reached through reading, listening, prayer and the conviction of the Holy Spirit by the church at large, would do much to alleviate the distress of those who feel judged and condemned by the church. And even where the conclusion reached is not favourably disposed toward divorce and remarriage, support, compassion and the all-encompassing, unconditional love of God should be paramount in the church in reaching out to the stepfamily.

Ruth, surely one of the most beautiful books of the Bible, tells the story of a successful stepfamily. The relationship between daughter-in-law and mother-in-law is an inspiration to all. We see in Naomi, as she prays God's blessing on each of her daughters-in-law and releases them to find new husbands after the death of her own sons, the unconditional and selfless quality of God's own love for us. The strength of that love is very evident as the younger women weepingly protest against the separation. But still Naomi, thinking only of their needs, insists that they return to their own people.

Only Ruth desists, movingly declaring her utter dedication to her mother-in-law, even to the extent of changing her own religion in favour of that of the older woman. But

* Cassettes available from Chichester Christian Fellowship. See appendix for address.

still Naomi, though accepting the allegiance of Ruth, puts the needs of her daughter-in-law before her own, as she urges her to seek marriage with her kinsman Boaz. The quality of Ruth's love for Naomi is obviously a testimony to all, as Boaz admits to having heard of all that she has done. 'May you be richly rewarded by the Lord, the God of Israel, under whose wings you have come to take refuge.'9 he said.

And as the story moves to a happy conclusion, we see God's blessing being worked out, and again being a testimony to many, as the women rejoice with Naomi at the birth of her first step-grandchild. (In actual fact the blood-tie lies only indirectly through Boaz). That this is an ongoing and successful step-relationship is very evident in the concluding verses and, perhaps most significantly, in the opening verses of Matthew where Boaz and Ruth appear in the genealogy of Jesus. God used a second marriage and stepfamily to bring about his greatest purpose!

No one would pretend that the modern stepfamily knows no problems. Yet Jesus own life was lived out in the context of a stepfamily, with Joseph his 'surrogate' father, and his brothers and sisters linked to him only through the blood of his mother.

Even for them, for Joseph and Mary, Jesus and his brothers, the problems were there, but by God's grace they were overcome. Joseph contemplated divorcing Mary quietly, unable, initially, to think of bringing up a child which was not his own: yet love overruled, conquering jealous pride, accepting, unequivocally, the message of the angel who told him 'do not be afraid to take Mary home as your wife, because what is conceived in her is from the Holy Spirit.'10

Mary herself held these things in her heart, pondering, wondering: she openly questioned Jesus' treatment of herself and Joseph (his stepfather) as they searched anxiously for him in the crowds after the Passover Feast in Jerusalem; and then came the quiet submission to all he said as she 'treasured all these things in her heart', despite her lack of understanding.[11]

Jesus' relationship with his brothers and the wider family too was not without its problems, as we recall their unbelief and his inability to perform miracles in their midst. 'Only in his home town among his relatives and in his own house is a prophet without honour,'[12] Jesus replied to their doubt and scorn.

The Bible gives clear guidelines as to the ideal in family relationships. From the story of the first family in Genesis, plus all the instruction of Proverbs and the Epistles, right through to the family of all families—Jesus' own—God highlights the importance of the family. The very fact that God chose the family unit as the means of bringing in the Saviour of the world puts the family in its rightful context—the foundation upon which the stability of society is founded.

Yet even a foundation needs a sound base upon which to be built. Jesus' own words to his parents when they remonstrated with him after having lost him in Jerusalem, give the key to the unshakable quality of that base: 'Didn't you know I had to be in my Father's house?'[13] Only when we, through Jesus the Son, know ourselves to be 'in the Father's house', will we have the assurance of having built our own house on terra firma—a foundation built on Jesus the Rock.

Whether you are building a first, or a second house, the words of Psalm 127:1 apply:

> Unless the Lord builds the house,
> the builders labour in vain.

Notes

1. Romans 8:1
2. 1 John 1:9
3. Luke 15:5, 6
4. Luke 15:7
5. John 8:7
6. 1 Timothy 3:2
7. Guy Duty, *Divorce and Remarriage*, published by Bethany Fellowship Inc, 6820 Auto Club Rd., Minneapolis, Minnesota, USA.
8. 2 Corinthians 5:17
9. Ruth 2:12
10. Matthew 1:20
11. Luke 2:51
12. Mark 6:4
13. Luke 2:49

Appendix

Chapter 6

Organisations offering residential weekend courses:

Association for Marriage Enrichment, 2 Overcliffe Rise, Southampton SO1 7BY.

Anglican Expression of Marriage Encounter, 9 College Close, Flamstead, St Albans, Herts AL3 8DJ; also 7 Lyons Close, Ruddington, Nottingham NG11 6BQ.

Baptist Expression of Marriage Encounter, 12 South Street, Leighton Buzzard, Beds LU7 8NT; also 26 Bellingdon Road, Chesham, Bucks HP5 2HA.

Marriage Fulfilment, 18 Lenton Road, The Park, Nottingham NG7 5DY.

Marriage Refreshment, Banks Farm, Barcombe, Lewes, Sussex BN8 5DY.

Marriage Review, 38 Park Drive, Ingatestone, Essex CM4 9DT.

Mission to Marriage, 20 Mill Street, Mildenhall, Suffolk 1P28 7DP.

Worldwide Marriage Encounter, England & Wales, 110 Lightwoods Road, Bearwood, Warley, West Midlands B67 5BH.

Chapter 12

Divorce (and Remarriage), parts 1 and 2, by Roger Price
   available from CCF Tapes, 30 Crescent Road, Bognor
   Regis, West Sussex PO21 1QG.

Conflict: Friend or Foe?
The creative use of conflict

by Joyce Huggett

'Like molten lava pouring from a volcano, conflict can burn up everything it falls upon, including potentially powerful relationships. The Christian church is littered with living testimonies of this sad fact.'

So says Joyce Huggett, who in this book explores ways of harnessing the energy generated in situations of conflict and turning it to creative use in God's purpose.

Through the principles shared here, marriages, friendships and church fellowships can find in conflict not an enemy to threaten but a friend to transform.

Joyce Huggett is a counsellor on the staff of St Nicholas' Church, Nottingham, and is well known for her books on marriage and relationships. She is married with two children.

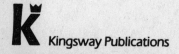

Kingsway Publications

Loneliness

by Elisabeth Elliot

There is nothing unique about loneliness. We have all experienced it, overtaking us when we least expect it. Loneliness engulfs us whether we're married, not-yet-married, or used-to-be-married. It comes in all stages of our lives, and we suffer in it.

Loneliness (not solitude) is nevertheless a gift. Through its wilderness God blazes a pathway to holiness—even joy. In it we realise fully the glorious meaning of the Cross of Christ. By it God can transform our wilderness into a watered garden.

Twice widowed, three times married, and having worked as a missionary in the rain forests of Ecuador, Elisabeth Elliot knows loneliness well. But in this lyrical and perceptive book she leads us beyond loneliness...to hope.

Also by Elisabeth Elliot in Kingsway paperback: *The Glad Surrender*.

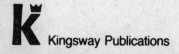

Kingsway Publications

Man to Man about Women

by James Dobson

It's time to be honest about ourselves. Today's society is involved in a pathetic search for personal pleasure.

Women's Lib is not so much a movement as a cry from the heart to be understood—as a God-given human being. Dr James Dobson attempts to set the matter right. He's a psychologist, husband and father. His writings are not theoretical but born of practical involvement in the problems confronted by women.

This book is for men and women—written by a man for men, but its aim is to understand one of God's greatest gifts to man—a woman!

Some of this book's topics—
    What causes depression in women
    The effect of fatigue and time pressure
    Sex machine or sex partner
    Menstrual and physiological problems
and a host of other down-to-earth factors.

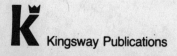

Kingsway Publications